Brookings at Seventy-Five

James Allen Smith

Brookings at Seventy-Five

THE BROOKINGS INSTITUTION

WASHINGTON D.C.

Copyright 1991 by
THE BROOKINGS INSTITUTION
1775 Massachusetts Avenue, N.W., Washington, D.C. 20036

Library of Congress Cataloging-in-Publication data

Smith, James Allen
Brookings at seventy-five / James Allen Smith.
   p.   cm.
Includes bibliographical references and index.
ISBN 0-8157-8008-7 (cloth)
1. Brookings Institution—History. 2. Policy
sciences—Research—United States—History. I. Title.
H67.W338S65 1991
001.4'06'073—dc20   90-22740
                             CIP

9 8 7 6 5 4 3 2 1

Credits for Photographs and Illustrations

Photographs of Robert Brookings; Robert Brookings and
Andrew Carnegie; the War Industries Board; Mr. and Mrs.
Robert Brookings; Jerome Green; Lewis Meriam, Leverett Lyon,
William Willoughby, and Edwin Nourse; Brookings graduates;
Leo Pasvolsky; Harold Moulton; the old Brookings building;
Kermit Gordon; and Henry Owen, courtesy of the Brookings
Institution Archives.

Photographs of Robert Calkins by Thomas L. Williams, Lyndon
Johnson and Robert Calkins by Reni Photos, and Arthur Okun
by Adams Studio, courtesy of the Brookings Institution Archives;
James Sundquist by Teresa Zabala, courtesy of the Brookings
Institution Public Affairs Office. Photographs of Alice M. Rivlin
by Laura Wulf; Henry Aaron by Stephen J. Sherman; and Friday
lunch by John Neubauer. Cartoons courtesy of *Barron's* and the
Cleveland Public Library.

Photographs of the new Brookings building; Bruce MacLaury;
Gilbert Y. Steiner; Joseph Pechman; Martha Derthick; Paul
Peterson; Thomas Mann; John Steinbruner; Charles L. Schultze;
James D. Carroll; A. Lee Fritschler; Lawrence J. Korb; and the
table group, courtesy of the Brookings Institution Public Affairs
Office.

CONTENTS

FOREWORD BY BRUCE MacLAURY   vii

PROLOGUE: GOVERNMENT AND CRITICAL
    INTELLIGENCE   I

1. WITH A VIEW TO PROMOTING
    EFFICIENCY   9

2. VOICE OF OPPOSITION   24

3. A THINK TANK COMES OF AGE   39

4. NEW AGENDAS   56

5. PUBLIC POLICY TOOLS   77

6. IMAGE AND IDEOLOGY   94

7. SHIFTING CENTERS   109

8. CONTINUITIES AND CHANGE   130

9. SETTING NEW AGENDAS   145

CONCLUSION: TOWARD INTELLIGENT
DEMOCRACY   163

NOTES   169

APPENDIXES

A. A BROOKINGS BIBLIOGRAPHY,
1966–90   175

B. BOARD OF TRUSTEES,
1916–91   205

C. FINANCIAL PROFILE,
1966–90   225

INDEX   229

ILLUSTRATIONS APPEAR BETWEEN
PAGES 46–47 AND 142–143

FOREWORD

AT ALL INSTITUTIONS, important anniversaries are cause for celebration—and the writing of histories. At Brookings, often considered the prototypical Washington research organization, the opportunity to look back over three quarters of a century of accomplishment was too alluring to resist.

In commissioning a history of the Brookings Institution for its seventy-fifth anniversary in 1991, we believed it crucial to engage an outside scholar to assess and document the impact of our chief product, our published research. James Allen Smith, a historian with a particular interest and expertise in the development and role of think tanks, has produced a book that brings an independent perspective to his subject. Although this history focuses on the past twenty-five years at Brookings, we hope that it will be a source of new insight into the interplay between public policy development and American academic institutions more generally.

Smith drew on his own considerable files on Brookings and other research institutions and was given complete access to the Brookings historical archives. This research was augmented by hundreds of interviews with past and present Brookings staff members and many outside sources as well. This process was key to the production of a volume that would be wide ranging as well as impartial.

The text is supplemented with appendixes listing all Brookings publications over the past twenty-five years, a complete catalog of members of the Brookings board of trustees since the institution began in 1916, and several charts tracing the institution's financial development.

Brookings at Seventy-Five is a successor volume to an earlier history by Charles B. Saunders, Jr., published in 1966, on the occasion of the institution's fiftieth anniversary. These chroniclings were not designed simply to record the achievements and conributions of the institution's past. Rather, they mark milestones along a path of discovery that reaches into the future. While we are proud of our legacy, our challenge now is to find the ways and means of extending this record to ensure that creative public policy research and education continues into the future.

The author wishes to express particular thanks to the program directors at Brookings who all gave unstintingly of their time, to John M. Hills, vice president for external affairs, and his staff, and to Robert L. Faherty, director of publications. The manuscript was edited by Theresa B. Walker and Caroline Lalire.

Funding for this project and other activities planned as part of the Brookings Institution's seventy-fifth anniversary was generously provided by the Ford Motor Company, and by ARCO, Bristol-Myers Squibb Company, CIGNA Corporation, and the Pacific Telesis Foundation.

The views expressed in this book are those of the author and should not be ascribed to those persons or organizations whose assistance is acknowledged or to the trustees, officers, or staff members of the Brookings Institution.

BRUCE K. MAC LAURY
President

January 1991
Washington, D.C.

Brookings at Seventy-Five

PROLOGUE:
GOVERNMENT AND
CRITICAL INTELLIGENCE

IN SEPTEMBER 1966, some one thousand notables from the worlds of academia, business, government, and philanthropy gathered to commemorate the Brookings Institution's fiftieth anniversary. Through the years Brookings had worked to bring the tools and findings of American social science research to bear on public policy issues. The institution's efforts had been steady—a stream of published studies, various conferences for government and corporate executives, training programs for graduate students, as well as countless quiet consultations with public officials. Despite shifts in Washington's policy climate and changes of presidential administrations, a deep-seated commitment to the practical usefulness of social science research had sustained the institution, linking its founders in the Progressive Era to the dignitaries who assembled a half century later.

The celebrations in 1966 symbolized a coming of age not merely for Washington's oldest policy research institution but for applied social science research as well. Many Americans had come to share the view that social science research could be of value to policymakers and the public. President John F. Kennedy's political appointments were widely hailed as marking a new era for academic specialists in government. President Lyndon B. Johnson, not a man reputed to be at home among professors and intellectuals, nonetheless turned to the nation's experts for help. He enthusiastically endorsed the use of social science as a tool for evaluating government programs.

After several months of negotiation between White House staff members and Brookings leaders, President Johnson agreed to speak at the Brookings celebration. It was an exceptional moment in the institution's history as a sitting president spoke about the often difficult relationship between government and what he called "critical intelligence." The president began his speech with praise for Brookings, recalling that he had been familiar with its reports as a young Democratic congressman in the 1930s (though diplomatically he left unspoken the institution's ardent opposition to several New Deal programs). He noted the institution's long-standing concerns with such practical, and ordinarily uncontentious, matters as the administrative organization and efficiency of federal agencies. He applauded the most recent Brookings research on transportation systems, civil service procedures, election law, labor relations, and the economy, saying that if the institution did not exist, "we would have to ask someone to create you."[1]

In publicly honoring the first half century of Brookings policy research and educational programs, Johnson also paid tribute to the nation's expanding social science research enterprise. He observed the growing numbers of policy research institutions across the country and praised the intellectual community's more general contributions to his Great Society programs. With characteristic grandeur he claimed that in preparing his legislative program he had personally examined "a thousand new ideas from the universities and research centers." He asserted that "without the tide of new proposals that periodically sweeps

into this city, the climate of our government would be very arid indeed."
The words were crafted by White House aide Harry McPherson but
the sentiments were apparently Johnson's, according to Robert Wood
who then served as secretary of the Department of Housing and Urban
Development.[2]

At the heart of his speech, Johnson addressed the broad question of
the place of knowledge in politics, defining three distinct kinds
of intellectual power—creating new ideas, administering complex
programs, and criticizing and evaluating policies. The first two intellectual powers, he thought, were in abundant supply, but the power to
evaluate was what the country most urgently needed at that moment.
He defined evaluation as the ability to say, "This works. But this does
not. This costs more than we can afford, or this costs more than it is
worth. This is worth more than it costs. This will probably give us an
acceptable result. But this will complicate the problem and make it
impossible for us to solve." His language resonated with the relatively
new quantitative formulations of the cost-benefit analyses and planning,
programming, and budgeting systems that had been introduced in
government agencies during his and his predecessor's administrations.

In the United States the effort to create a serviceable social science
and to persuade political leaders to enlist social scientists in government
service had proceeded fitfully since before the turn of the century.
During that long endeavor Brookings had been the pioneering institution in Washington. Its history parallels the history of applied social
science research and the arrival of social science expertise as a force in
American policymaking.[3] By the time of Lyndon Johnson's administration, social scientists had won an apparently secure place in dozens of
government research and advisory agencies. Government funding for
research and evaluation seemed virtually limitless, often having been
mandated when new programs were created. Plans for new graduate
programs in applied social science and public policy were also in the
works at a number of universities. And celebratory talk about "the end

of ideology" and the beginnings of "the knowledgeable society" had a convincing ring as one looked at the many experts in government and sensed the tacit political consensus underpinning Johnson's legislative agenda.

But the moment of optimism and self-congratulation among social scientists and policymakers proved to be short-lived. Johnson's speech had an edge to it. He hinted ominously at the mounting tension between intellectuals and his administration. Indeed, fissures had recently widened between the president and the intellectual community as the military buildup in Vietnam proceeded. Those tensions had contributed in part to the resignation only a few weeks earlier of a presidential adviser, Princeton historian Eric Goldman, who served as Johnson's liaison with the academic community.[4] And within the White House, the president and some of his advisers worried that domestic legislation had moved so fast that new programs were already spinning out of control.

In retrospect, Johnson's appeal for critical evaluation—"precise," "sharp," and "piercing" were the qualities he attached to the critical faculty—signaled a turning point. Not only were individual policies and programs going to be put to the explicit tests of critical analysis, but so also were the premises that had undergirded American social and economic reform since the Progressive Era. Social scientists would soon embark on an agonizing reappraisal of their contributions to Great Society programs. Their intellectual torment would be prolonged into the 1970s by the baffling economic phenomenon of "stagflation" and recriminations over the nation's misadventure in Vietnam. At the same time, ideological challenges were being mounted from right and left, casting into grave doubt both the idea of unbiased social science research and the role played by experts in the policy process.

Johnson's speech to the Brookings audience probably marked the crest of governmental and academic confidence in rational analytic techniques of policy planning and evaluation. Long-standing American hopes that social science research could be disinterested, nonpartisan, and an antidote to ideological divisiveness soon gave way to one of the most partisan and ideologically charged epochs in twentieth-century American history. The political center did not hold. And for Brookings, an institution that through much of its history had helped to define the operative middle ground in American politics, the 1970s and 1980s presented challenges unforeseen by those who celebrated its first half century in 1966. Fundamental assumptions about the relationship between knowledge and politics were called into question. The always tenuous links between research and political decisionmaking grew more fragile. Even the prestige of the policy expert—the "action intellectual" in Theodore White's resonant phrase from the mid-1960s—plummeted. As the tenor of the nation's public policy discourse became more heated and divisive, the value of social science research and the possibility of dispassionate discourse about the issues confronting the nation were thrown into question.

Twenty-five years have passed since Johnson's speech. In 1991 Brookings can look back proudly on having completed another quarter century of public policy research, publishing, and education. On the occasion of its seventy-fifth anniversary, celebration is in order as it was in 1966. But it is inevitably somewhat tempered by events. America's faith in social science as an instrument of policy guidance has evaporated since the 1960s; so too have many of the intellectual certainties that once shaped our views of government's domestic role and the paramount place of the United States in the international order. Confidence in the capacity of our political and economic institutions to function wisely and well has also diminished sharply. And experts as a group have been found wanting. This Brookings anniversary is a fitting time to reflect about our accumulated knowledge of government, the economy, and international affairs and of the part an institution such as Brookings has played—and ought to play—in the nation's public affairs.

At its founding Brookings was singularly well positioned to contribute to the public policymaking process. In 1916 government research agencies and private research institutes were few; expert advisory mechanisms for both the executive and legislative branches were informal; graduate training and university research in the social sciences was in its adolescence; and philanthropic support for research on social and economic issues was directed toward a relatively small universe of research centers.

At the age of seventy-five, however, Brookings operates in a vastly different environment from the one it operated in even at its fiftieth anniversary. In recent years, the universe of Washington-based policy research organizations has been transformed. Scores of new private research institutions have been founded—some engaged in solid research in specialized policy areas, some advocacy-oriented, some avowedly ideological, some working under contract to government and private clients. The policymaking environment has also changed with vast improvements in the federal government's capacities for research. New government research bodies were set up in the 1970s, including the Congressional Budget Office and Office of Technology Assessment, and various research and evaluation units in cabinet departments. The policy research capabilities of older groups such as the Office of Management and Budget (known early on as the Bureau of the Budget), the General Accounting Office, and the Congressional Research Service (successor to the older Legislative Reference Service) were expanded and strengthened.

Operating with relatively little competition as recently as twenty-five years ago, Brookings now toils in a crowded arena. Yet it still stands out, differing in obvious respects from government research agencies and in less clear-cut but no less significant ways from the many private organizations that now share the imprecise, colloquial designation "think tank." The age and stability of Brookings set it apart; in fact, two-thirds of Washington's roughly one hundred think tanks are less than twenty years old and only a handful have budgets in the $15 to $20 million range of Brookings. Although small when measured against the staffs of some government research units, its staff of more than two hundred, about one-quarter of whom are senior scholars, is among the largest and most diverse of private American think tanks, exceeded in size and budget only by a few large contract research organizations. With a publishing program that sees some twenty-five books, two economics journals, and a more popularly oriented policy quarterly into print each year, Brookings also works as a moderate-sized publishing house. Brookings is also engaged in a rare type of postgraduate education, offering a curriculum of public policy programs geared primarily toward government officials and private sector executives. The academic strength of its staff, the diversity of research projects and educational offerings, and the scale of its publishing program make Brookings one of the few freestanding policy research centers that can operate on a par with the nation's major research universities.

Moreover, with an endowment in excess of $90 million, which now supplies more than 25 percent of its annual budget, Brookings is also one of the very few policy research centers to have a margin of financial autonomy. And unlike many of the nation's largest think tanks, Brookings takes few government research contracts; they now account for only 1 percent of its revenues. Although Brookings must still rely for financial support on foundations, corporations, and individual donors, it is freer than any other nonuniversity policy research institution from reliance on a single category of support. Insulated to a degree from the demands of short-term projects and the relentless, time-consuming search for funding, Brookings scholars have often been able to pursue research with a longer horizon than electoral cycles and legislative calendars.

The Brookings Institution offers a vantage point from which to observe the changing relationship between expert knowledge and political decisionmaking in our democracy. While the old ideals of nonpartisanship, disinterested expertise, and critical detachment formulated by Progressive-Era reformers may seem quaintly outmoded in modern Washington, Brookings still seeks to give those ideals contemporary meaning. In the 1960s Eugene D. Black, then chairman of the Brookings board, observed that "illuminating all the choices is the fundamental purpose of research."[5] If self-government is about making informed choices and grappling realistically with the consequences of our decisions, then few research or educational institutions have been so long engaged in advancing our democratic experiment.

1
WITH A VIEW TO
PROMOTING EFFICIENCY

ALEXIS DE TOCQUEVILLE marveled long ago at the "intellectual and moral associations of the Americans," observing how routine it was for individuals who shared a common opinion or goal to organize a society, a movement, or a group. Even the stolid Washington research institution that through much of its history has embodied intellectual detachment and scholarly expertise can trace its beginnings to the passionate embrace of an idea. The founders of the small research institute that became the Brookings Institution were proponents of a powerful movement that now arouses few passions and only faintly resonates across the decades. Yet it captured the imagination—tapping the organizing abilities and opening the pocketbooks—of surprisingly large numbers of reform-minded citizens in the early 1900s. They were advocates of the cause of economy and efficiency in government, crusading to place government activities on a sound businesslike basis, and to do so through research.

Founding Ideals

Rooted in the principles of scientific management first introduced by Frederick Winslow Taylor in the 1880s, the government efficiency movement united practically inclined reformers, businessmen, and social scientists who were disillusioned with the high-minded moralistic tone of earlier campaigns for good government. Instead, they placed their faith in research, expertise, and administrative competence. In scores of cities around the country, civic groups established government research bureaus geared toward making city agencies more efficient. The most famous, the New York Bureau of Municipal Research, was incorporated in 1907. Out of its success at the city level, the Institute for Government Research, forerunner of the Brookings Institution, soon took shape in Washington.[1]

At the core of the efficiency movement was a sincere conviction that political administration could be both nonpartisan and scientific. As they looked at boss-dominated urban political machines and heard the clamor of mass politics, the backers of government research bureaus felt that society would be better governed if the administrative domain of public life were expanded and the political domain reduced. In truth, they watched partisan politics at the turn of the century with a mixture of worry, fear, and contempt, preferring to place their political hopes in scientific and managerial expertise.

The calls for greater municipal government efficiency echoed in Washington, and in 1910 President William Howard Taft persuaded Congress to appropriate $100,000 to set up a presidential Commission on Economy and Efficiency. Its charge was to look into the financial and accounting practices of federal agencies. After two years of study it recommended the creation of a new federal budget process centered in the executive branch.[2] Although the idea received bipartisan endorsement, it stalled under President Woodrow Wilson in 1913. Its proponents soon began working to organize an independent Institute for Government Research, intending to give budget legislation—and the nonpartisan administrative ethos it represented—a boost.

The institute's organizers knew intimately the realms of research, government service, and philanthropy. Among the prime movers, three men stand out. Frederick Cleveland, a founder of the New York Bureau of Municipal Research and director of Taft's Economy Commission, is most often credited with originating the idea for a research institute in Washington. Charles D. Norton, a banker and Taft's private secretary (a post that would be more like today's special assistant to the president), gave the research institute plans an enthusiastic and authoritative push when he returned to New York in 1913. Jerome D. Greene, a lawyer and secretary of the newly established Rockefeller Foundation, brought his knowledge of philanthropy to the enterprise. With Norton's help, Greene worked out a structure and financing for the new institute.

Greene's 1915 prospectus for the institute spoke forthrightly of government as a business, arguing that it must be run efficiently and economically. This was not a partisan cause for Greene, who saw "no difference of opinion among good citizens as to the urgent necessity for efficiency and intelligent economy in administration." He was also convinced that studies of government were most effective when undertaken by private groups or a "citizens' organization." "Such studies, to command public confidence, must be beyond suspicion of having a partisan or personal aspect," he wrote, explaining that governmental commissions "are almost certainly to arouse political discussions or inter-departmental jealousies."[3] To convince the public that the organization's aims were not partisan or politically motivated, Greene and Norton invited a number of distinguished people to serve as trustees "with the frank statement that their chief function was to vouch before the public for the integrity of the enterprise and its freedom from the slightest political bias."[4]

When the new Institute for Government Research was formally incorporated in March 1916, its board included a mixture of businessmen

and academics, liberals and conservatives, easterners and westerners—
a relatively diverse group by the standards of the era, even to the point
of including one woman, Mrs. Edward H. Harriman. There were
recognizably conservative members with practical business perspectives
such as railroad executive James J. Hill, financier R. Fulton Cutting,
American Telephone and Telegraph executive Theodore Vail, and the
conservative economist and Yale University president Arthur Twining
Hadley. There were others with strong academic ties such as Harvard's
esteemed former president Charles W. Eliot, his successor A. Lawrence
Lowell, Carnegie Institution president Robert Woodward, and Johns
Hopkins president Frank Goodnow, who was one of the nation's most
distinguished scholars of public administration and, fittingly, chosen as
the institute's chairman. There were also recognizable liberals and
reformers such as Harvard law professor Felix Frankfurter and University of Wisconsin president Charles R. van Hise. A less well-known
businessman from St. Louis, Robert S. Brookings, served as vice
chairman.

The cause that united them was administrative efficiency. It was not
a movement designed to rouse political passions, but that in part was
the point. Government, from day to day, was not a matter of emotion
but of quiet competence and professionalism. Although they did not
march beneath banners, the bold capital letters of a pamphlet announc-
ing the creation of the Institute for Government Research served in
place of shorter slogans and credos: "An Association of Citizens for
Co-operating with Public Officials in the Scientific Study of Business
Methods with a View to Promoting Efficiency in the National Government and Advancing the Science of Administration."[5]

Forty-three donors pledged $160,000 to see the new Institute for
Government Research through its first five years. It opened its doors
in October 1916, occupying a red-brick building at 818 Connecticut
Avenue. A staff of six researchers, most of them former civil servants
with solid academic credentials, went to work under the direction of

William F. Willoughby, a professor of politics and jurisprudence at Princeton who had earlier held government posts in Puerto Rico and also served on the Taft Commission.

Much of the institute's early work was pursued quietly and routinely. The staff helped governmental agencies with the mundane work of improving their administrative procedures. They advised agencies on setting up modern accounting systems, creating office files, and drafting personnel manuals. The essence of its work for more than a decade was to help each agency bring its administrative routines into line with modern business methods. Throughout the 1920s the institute's publications included important but less than scintillating titles: *Principles Governing the Retirement of Public Employees* (1918), *The Federal Service: A Study of the System of Personnel Administration of the United States Government* (1922), *Reorganization of the Administrative Branch of the National Government* (1923), *The Statistical Work of the National Government* (1925), and *Manual of Accounting and Reporting for the Operating Services of the National Government* (1926). The steady flow of publications and constant consulting with government agencies helped transform accounting practices and civil service hiring and administration in the interwar years.

During the 1920s, the institute also prepared administrative monographs, some sixty in all, examining the efficiency of individual agencies of the federal government. They treated large and small agencies alike, providing a comprehensive view of which agencies were doing what, how they exercised their responsibilities, and where there might be duplication and waste. In surveying government departments, tedious as the work now appears, the institute's scholars were collecting the facts and data that they hoped would create a foundation for a more rigorous science of public administration as well as a more professional civil service. At the same time they were devising standards and measures of efficiency against which citizens could begin to judge the work of government officials.

The institute's most noteworthy early success—the first chapter in the Brookings Institution's continuing interest in the federal budget process—was in advancing the cause of budget reform. Without a centralized, executive-controlled budget process at the federal level, there was little prospect of controlling or curtailing government spending. A passel of congressional committees competed with one another, creating a chaotic and expensive process. The Budget and Accounting Act of 1921 finally fulfilled on the national level the hopes of the Taft Commission members who had sought a more rational budget process. President Warren G. Harding heralded the legislation as "the greatest reform in governmental practices since the beginning of the republic."

While the general contours of an executive budget process had been laid out years earlier by the Taft Commission, the Institute for Government Research remained busy at every stage of the legislative process, drafting House and Senate versions of the budget reform bill, organizing congressional testimony, and arranging publicity to generate support for its passage. After the bill became law, the administrative tasks in setting up the Bureau of the Budget were undertaken by the institute as well, even to the point of housing the fledgling bureau and providing staff until it could secure its own offices and personnel.

The passage of budget legislation and the admittedly tedious administrative work in Washington meant that some of the early enthusiasm for the institute inevitably diminished. With initial financial support running out, the institute faced an uncertain future. Its seventy-year-old vice chairman, Robert S. Brookings, once described as a "benign human steam engine," turned his extraordinary energies to keeping the institute alive through the 1920s (raising $300,000 in a two-month period in 1920) and molding a far more ambitious research enterprise.

Brookings the Builder

Robert Brookings had been drawn to Washington and initiated into the day-to-day workings of government during World War I. Serving on the War Industries Board along with Bernard Baruch and Robert S. Lovett, Brookings, like other "dollar a year" business executives, was often frustrated by the complexities of mobilizing the nation's resources for war and coordinating national economic activities. He and his colleagues on the board were especially troubled by the deficiencies of economic data. Brookings remained in Washington after the war, eager to put to work some of the lessons he derived from his tenure on the board.

Almost certainly his wartime service strengthened his commitment to the Institute for Government Research and its quest for more efficient government. It also sparked an interest in improving economic research and creating a better-trained corps of civil servants. But the Institute for Government Research was not an ample enough vehicle for his various schemes. In the early 1920s he restlessly pursued new plans for a separate economic research institute and a new training school to prepare students for careers in public service.

Brookings's involvement in the research institution that came to bear his name covers only the final chapters of a remarkable life. Born in Maryland in 1850, he left school at sixteen and followed his brother to St. Louis, where he put rudimentary bookkeeping skills to work with the firm of Cupples and Marston. As manufacturers and distributors of various household goods—clothespins, twine, brooms, and woodenware—they found expansive markets as American settlers migrated westward after the Civil War. Brookings, toting a violin along with his sample case, was the firm's most successful traveling salesman, wandering a territory that extended from the Mississippi River to the Pacific Ocean. He earned a partnership in the firm by the age of twenty-one, the post of principal manager in his late twenties, and accumulated a fortune of more than $6 million by the time he left the business in his mid-forties. He was tough in a rough-and-tumble business environment, remarking late in life that both he and his competitors would have been put in jail for the practices they had engaged in during the 1870s and 1880s.

While capable of rolling over business rivals and cannily outmaneuvering much larger business trusts, he always seemed to long for something more. Acutely sensitive about his lack of formal education and refinement, he asked local college professors to compile reading lists and sought tutoring on matters of grammar and etiquette from members of the St. Louis social circles he aspired to join. From a relatively early age he seemed ambivalent about the ultimate value of his business career. He traveled several times to Europe, once to explore social service experiments in England and on another extended sabbatical to discover whether his amateur musical talents showed professional promise (a Berlin teacher told him they did not). At forty-six, mentally exhausted from his business ventures, he decided to devote his remaining years to other projects.

His wealth had given him access to educational and philanthropic circles in St. Louis, and he became president of the board of Washington University. Although it was then an ailing college of fewer than one hundred students, his fund raising and business sense transformed it into one of the region's principal universities. His interests in higher education led to a friendship with Andrew Carnegie, who opened even wider national and international vistas for him. He became a trustee of the Carnegie Corporation, the Carnegie Endowment for International Peace, and the Smithsonian Institution.

He was, by all accounts, a tireless talker, wearying any number of his listeners. "His lightness was inclined to be awkward, his persiflage had no yeast in it. . . . Frequently he wandered far from the point," wrote his biographer. But his loquaciousness served him well when it came to raising money. "He would tackle anyone for money," a friend commented, "and if you had any that wasn't nailed down, Brookings would be likely to get it. He was resourceful, steady, determined, he never let up on a man; and just wore people out."[6] When he traveled the country in the 1920s raising money for the institute in Washington, he argued over and over that the only way to reduce the federal wartime deficit was to make government more efficient. At all times, his deep commitments to Washington University and the Brookings Institution were, so it seemed to observers, practically motivated. "Mr. Brookings never revealed any emotional basis for his interest in social welfare, he was not a professional uplifter," recalled the institution's president in 1950, "he always retained a sense of realism."[7]

Like others who had participated in the wartime economic mobilization—and been surprised at the hitherto untapped productive strength of the national economy—he came to be convinced that economic research could be a powerful policy tool. "It is self-evident," he asserted, "that the modern economic system has many defects, many sources of waste and friction, and that the annual avoidable economic losses are stupendous in amount."[8] Economic research would ferret out the sources of waste and inefficiency. In 1922 he approached his friend Henry Pritchett, then serving as head of the Carnegie Corporation, with an idea for an economic research institution. It would not engage in basic economic research; the three-year-old National Bureau of Economic Research under Wesley Mitchell already had staked out a claim as a center for theoretical work. Instead, the institute Brookings envisioned would assemble and interpret economic data for the use of policymakers and the public.

The Carnegie Corporation staff agreed with Brookings's plans and committed $1.65 million over the next ten years to an Institute of Economics. From the beginning the new institute was viewed as a companion of the older Institute for Government Research; within a few months of its founding they were sharing quarters in a new building on Jackson Place, near Lafayette Square.

Harold G. Moulton, an economist specializing in banking and finance, left the University of Chicago to direct the new institute. The thirty-nine-year-old professor saw it as a risky venture. He was wary of a research institution with so many businessmen on its board. He worried about the constraints of seeking philanthropic support for scholarly research. And he bluntly told Robert Brookings that he did not want to manage an organization that would simply operate as a front for business interests; he did not intend to lead a trade association or business research group. As inducement to head the institute, Moulton received explicit, written guarantees that the research program would be in the hands of the director. The trustees' primary function was "not to express their views on the scientific investigations conducted by the Institute, but only to make it possible for such scientific work to be done under the most favorable auspices."[9] That early statement of policy would continue to define the lines of responsibility, with trustees setting out broad policy guidelines and seeing to the financial well-being of the institution while the research directors and staff members shaped the specific research program and took individual responsibility for the published books and reports.

The growing professionalization of social science research was already apparent in the 1920s, and, over the years, professional specialization has reinforced the relative autonomy of researchers from board direction and control. Moulton, one of the most outspoken professional economists of his day, was confident that the discipline of economics was well on its way toward becoming a science. He would tolerate no interference in the research enterprise from the laymen on the board.

Moulton assembled a dozen-member team of professional economists, including Edwin Nourse, an agricultural economist who would later serve as the first chairman of the Council of Economic Advisers;

Isador Lubin, a pioneering economic statistician who had worked on the War Industries Board; Leo Pasvolsky, a specialist in international economics who would head the State Department's research operations during World War II; and Thomas Walker Page, a former member of the Tariff Commission who worked on international trade issues.

In the 1920s the research program of the Institute of Economics focused on the problems of postwar economic reconstruction and reparations, international trade, agriculture, and labor policy. Its studies of war debts and reparations pointedly argued that reparations were undermining the German economy and that interallied war debts would have to be scaled down. Studies of tariff policies demonstrated the detrimental economic consequences of pursuing a restrictive trade regime. Despite the institute's warnings, U.S. policy culminated in the 1930 Smoot-Hawley tariff.

Unlike their colleagues in the Institute for Government Research, who were interested in the administrative efficiency of government agencies, the economists in the Institute of Economics were concerned more broadly with the efficiency of the national and international economy. They looked not at administrative procedures but at the likely consequences of specific policies. They quickly learned that intellectual insight and rigorous research do not by themselves animate the policy process, let alone shape policy outcomes. The linkages between the realms of research and policymaking were still relatively undeveloped. In the 1920s there were as yet few permanent governmental advisory and planning mechanisms to channel research findings into the policy process and to digest them for elected officials and other policymakers. Although Herbert Hoover, first as secretary of commerce and later as president, experimented with countless ad hoc advisory commissions, the modern networks of policy expertise and advising had only begun to take shape. The Council of Economic Advisers, National Security Council, specialized congressional research agencies and committee staffs, and other policy research bodies were later inventions. And they could emerge only when sufficient numbers of people had received professional training in the relevant academic disciplines and only if political leaders were persuaded of the value of research. Early on, Robert Brookings sensed the need for more sophisticated and better-trained cadres in public service.

A Training School for Public Service

As president of Washington University's board of trustees, Robert Brookings had witnessed revolutionary changes in American graduate and professional training around the turn of the century. The complexity of life in a newly urban, industrial nation required better-educated and more skillful professionals in all kinds of fields. New graduate schools in business, law, medicine, social work, and public administration were founded in many universities, while old graduate programs underwent fundamental reform.

Robert Brookings was among a number of people who saw the need for better-trained civil servants, whether that training was in public administration, law, or social science. But as a businessman he did not invoke lofty notions of civic duty or public service when he thought about their vocation. Efficiency was the standard. "This government," he asserted, "whose powers are becoming broader and whose functions are becoming more complex, demands efficient workers."

His commitment to training people for government work led him to endow a department of economics and government at Washington University in 1923. Wary of the consequences of the increasing specialization of academic life and the growing research orientation of university social science departments, he wanted to be sure that any curriculum for prospective government workers would include practical experience in the day-to-day problems of government. He arranged to bring students from St. Louis to Washington, D.C., for part of their training.

Their work would be overseen by the research staffs of the Institute for Government Research and the Institute for Economics. However, when the arrangement ran afoul of Missouri's laws governing nonprofit organizations, the graduate program had to be reincorporated in the District of Columbia in 1924 as the Robert S. Brookings Graduate School. He endowed it with enough money to yield between $40,000 and $50,000 a year. Isabel Vallé January, his long-time friend and wife-to-be, gave $350,000 and George Eastman of Eastman Kodak also pledged $50,000 a year for seven years. Closely linked to the two research institutes, the graduate school shared board members and drew upon research staff members as faculty.

The graduate school proved to be only a short-lived educational experiment—successful when the roster of its distinguished graduates is read, a failure when measured against the hopes of its founder. Robert Brookings wanted "to teach the art of handling problems rather than to impart accumulated knowledge . . . and . . . to turn out craftsmen who can make contributions to an intelligent direction of social change."[10] But practical, problem-focused training could not survive in the face of the discipline-bound, research-oriented training of the nation's most prestigious graduate programs. Nor did the school's curriculum, under the direction of Dean Walton Hamilton, ever live up to Brookings's expectations. Hamilton, who had taught at Amherst College, built a program without formal courses and credits, but one that emphasized history, philosophy, and political theory. These were not, in the founder's view, the basis of practical training. To the dismay of Robert Brookings and especially the research staff of the Institute for Government Research, the students demonstrated little interest in assisting with the preparation of personnel manuals, analyzing accounting methods, or writing administrative histories of federal agencies.

Despite an enthusiastic body of graduate students, many of whom did choose governmental careers, the graduate school foundered within a few years. Brookings thought the problem was "that the granting of a doctor's degree has had a tendency to bring us less mature students . . . who have had primarily in mind a teaching career, the universities of the country having made such a degree almost an ultimatum in their teaching requirements." The school, he confessed, was "a long way in its results from the direct service I have always had in mind."[11]

In fact, the issues were more fundamental. There were serious disputes within the three institutions about the kinds of training and expertise that would offer the best grounding for government service and the analysis of public policy. Walton Hamilton, with his interest in history and political theory, placed the emphasis on politics, broadly interpreted as the study of political thought and institutions. He complained that the Institute for Government Research did not study government, politics, or policy, but was too narrowly focused on administrative matters. In concerning itself with economy and efficiency, he wrote, "it takes agencies for granted and avoids questions of reason for existence and of function."[12] Hamilton's views posed a challenge to an institute where "administrative science" was based on the conviction that politics and administration, borrowing Woodrow Wilson's early distinction, were separate spheres. Less directly, he challenged Moulton's view that social science, primarily economics, could be the foundation for a disinterested, scientific approach to public policymaking.

Tensions between Hamilton's approach to graduate training and the applied research programs of the two institutes were compounded by the cumbersome administrative structure linking three nominally distinct organizations—all under the overall guidance of Robert Brookings, who chaired the boards and raised the funds. Serious discussions about merging them began in 1926 and were completed and approved by the three boards in December 1927. Unable to reconcile the teaching and research operations—and forced to acknowledge that American graduate education was increasingly specialized and discipline-oriented—the graduate school was phased out, although Ph.D.'s continued to be awarded well into the 1930s until altogether some seventy-four doctorates were granted. A modest "training division" continued to bring in graduate and postgraduate fellows from other institutions until World War II depleted the ranks of university graduate programs. The merger and reorganization set a general course for the institution. The unified institution took the name of its indefatigable builder and benefactor, Robert Brookings, who served as chairman of the board until his death in 1932. Moulton was chosen as its first president, a post he held until 1952. Under his leadership the institution was primarily a center of applied research, serving as an intellectual bridge between universities and government. But its relationships with academic social scientists were not always comfortable. Researchers at Brookings were concerned about the "narrowing specialization" of the university, arguing that it "has had a tendency to render social science, as a whole, increasingly impotent in the service of society."[13] Moulton and his staff saw the institution as both an adjunct and a counterweight to the university, a place where interdisciplinary policy research could be undertaken, scholarly collaboration fostered, and practical postgraduate work offered.

The ethos of nonpartisan research still shaped the researchers' sense of mission. They addressed national policy concerns but aimed to do so "independently of the special interests of any group in the body politic, either political, social or economic." As long as the research had focused primarily on narrow questions of administrative efficiency, nonpartisanship was an easy concept to uphold. But the difficulties of defining "nonpartisanship" and remaining above the political fray were soon to become apparent in the politically charged decade of the 1930s. Society was torn by the Great Depression. The policy orthodoxies of the 1920s no longer seemed to work, and a president avowedly committed to "bold, persistent experimentation" began to redefine the scope of federal policymaking. The role of the independent policy research institute would begin to change.

2 VOICE OF OPPOSITION

IN THE 1910S AND 1920S the institutions operating under Robert Brookings's umbrella earned intellectual respect for their painstaking administrative studies and careful work on the budget process, tariff policy, agriculture, and war debts. However, widespread public recognition eluded the institution for the most part. In fact, the moment of greatest public notice (and notoriety) came immediately after the founding of the Institute for Government Research. Some observers, aware that the Rockefeller Foundation had provided financial support to organizers of the institute, called it the "Rockefeller Inquiry." Somehow they viewed the infant organization as John D. Rockefeller's revenge for both the government antitrust case that broke up the Standard Oil Trust and the investigations into Rockefeller business practices. The research organization, so new and unfamiliar, troubled populists fearful of the ways big business might influence political decisions in Washington. Nonetheless, the hue and cry in the popular press quieted down almost as soon as the institute began its mundane administrative research and consulting.

During the 1930s, however, Brookings made a considerable name for itself, earning a reputation as a locus of opposition to Franklin D. Roosevelt's recovery and reform programs. Later commentators recognized Brookings as a bitter opponent of Harry Truman's efforts to expand the New Deal's social agenda. Hugh Johnson, who headed Roosevelt's National Recovery Administration, assailed the Brookings criticisms of the National Industrial Recovery Act, describing the institution as "one of the most sanctimonious and pontifical rackets in the country." He attacked its research, complaining that there ought to be a "penal statute for people who pervert plain facts to the injury of the public."[1] Stuart Chase, one of the most widely read economic journalists of the era, said in more tepid words, "From time to time it looks up from its adding machines and logarithmic curves long enough to hurl a treatise, most uncomplimentary to the New Deal, in the general direction of the White House."[2] According to a labor publication, Brookings was "a research center which usually assembles a lot of rubber facts to prove that the planks in the Republican Party platform are based on natural and divine law."[3] The popular image of Brookings for some twenty years after Roosevelt's arrival in Washington remained that of a predominantly Republican, conservative, and business-oriented institution. The *Nation* denounced Brookings as "the outstanding servant of reaction in America."[4]

But image and reality are often intertwined in complex ways. Ideological and partisan labels tend to oversimplify research and policy recommendations and often fail to grasp the subtle relationships between outside policy experts and government officials. In 1932 Brookings president Harold Moulton and many of his colleagues had apparently been eager to see a Democratic victory and were ready to join ranks behind Roosevelt. Despite Herbert Hoover's long association with the scientific management movement, Roosevelt had seemed the more inventive presidential candidate and the one better able to lead the nation out of its deepening economic crisis. Moreover, the New York governor had a reputation, dating from his stint as assistant secretary of the navy, as a disciple of administrative reform. His 1932 campaign pronouncements on balanced budgets and government economy served as welcome reassurances to the economists and administrative experts working at Brookings.

With the president's uncle, Frederic A. Delano, a board member since 1920 and chairman following Robert Brookings's death in 1932, the opportunities for direct government service seemed limitless. Delano volunteered—and Roosevelt eagerly accepted—the institution's services in the expected campaign for government economizing that would follow the inauguration. Consequently, Brookings staff members advised the Roosevelt appointees in the Budget Bureau and Commerce Department on budget cuts and reorganization during the trying winter of 1933. Yet in an early signal of Roosevelt's capacity to dismiss expert advice and change policy direction abruptly, the proposals for government economizing never came to fruition.

After the onset of the depression Brookings had to confront its own debilitating budget cuts. Dependent on large foundations and individual donors for its annual budget of roughly $300,000 in 1930, the institution had plunged into dire financial trouble by the time Roosevelt took office. The Carnegie Corporation's ten-year grant for the economics program expired in 1931 and was not renewed; a seven-year commitment from the Laura Spelman Rockefeller Memorial for the support of public administration research ended; and Robert Brookings, having given approximately $1 million during his lifetime, had made it clear before his death in 1932 that no more resources would soon be forthcoming from him or his estate. The financial prospects during the depression were so gloomy that the terms of a $2 million matching grant from the Rockefeller Foundation could not be satisfied.

With only $30,000 in annual income generated from the endowment (about 10 percent of its annual budget), Moulton, never a man eager to ask individuals for money, had to cut back the research program. He also shifted toward a bolder investment policy, investing in stocks (a strategy then deemed highly risky by most endowed institutions) and constructing and managing Washington office buildings. By the late 1930s he had steered the institution through the depression's worst dangers.

To save the research program, however, Brookings undertook contract research for government and private clients. Building on state surveys they had done in the 1920s, the staff advised several state governments on cost-cutting measures, taxation, and reorganization. They also did consulting work for such groups as the Chamber of Commerce, the National Tax Association, and the American Federation of Labor. The institution's long-term interest in transportation and regulatory issues can be traced to a study of the nation's transportation system undertaken for the National Transportation Committee, a group headed by Calvin Coolidge and funded largely by financial institutions with heavy investments in railroads. Out of necessity, the institution accepted virtually every paying project that came its way during the depression.

While contract-research reports and public administration mono-graphs continued to issue from Brookings, Moulton and his colleagues also began a series of critical appraisals of New Deal programs, focusing especially on the National Recovery Administration and the Agricultural Adjustment Administration. The early rapport with the New Dealers soon gave way to sometimes bitter hostility.

In 1933 Moulton had had access to the inner circles where economic recovery legislation was being debated. He drafted his own version of a recovery bill and urged Delano to take it directly to the president. Moulton was then invited to join a drafting committee that was working under the auspices of Senator Robert Wagner of New York. As the drafting process moved forward, the National Industrial Recovery bill looked less and less like the legislation Moulton had envisioned. Its price-setting arrangements bestowed more power on government price-fixers than Moulton thought economically prudent. After the legislation passed in June 1933, he and his Brookings colleagues, principally Leverett Lyon, embarked on a highly critical series of studies of the National Recovery Administration. They concluded that the NRA had actually impeded recovery.

Moulton, Lyon, and other Brookings economists were wary of federal meddling with market mechanisms, whether it came through NRA-sanctioned cartels or the price supports and crop allocation arrangements of the Agricultural Adjustment Administration.

The Brookings studies of the NRA and the AAA were primarily the work of economists. They were also inspired by Edwin Nourse's interest in "concurrent history," using what social scientists were then calling the "capture and record" method. In a sense they were rudimentary exercises in program evaluation, looking at administrative problems and at the economic impact of the programs under review.

The NRA volumes proved controversial in ways the older administrative studies had never been. Brookings criticisms of the NRA anticipated disputes within the NRA as well as popular discontent with the recovery measures. The critical tone of the Brookings studies prompted the president to appoint a cabinet committee to reappraise the NRA and supplied ammunition for the NRA's opponents on Capitol Hill. Ultimately, a Supreme Court decision in 1935 declared the National Industrial Recovery Act unconstitutional.

Generally less critical than the NRA analysis, the AAA studies undertaken by Edwin Nourse were welcomed by the secretary of agriculture for the administrative problems they identified and their general endorsement of the AAA as a needed response to the economic emergency. The studies warned, however, that paying farmers to limit their crop acreage was not a sound long-term policy.

Moulton clearly saw the dangers such critical research posed for an institution that wanted to maintain cordial relations with federal officials. Having felt the heat for the studies of the NRA, he was leery of releasing the AAA study. He knew that it would stir up controversy in the election year of 1936. The publication of the study was delayed until 1937, with Moulton expressing the hope that it would serve as a guide to future agricultural policy and not as an instrument of partisan controversy.

Indeed, despite Moulton's often blustery tone of disapproval at what he saw as unwarranted New Deal interventions in the market, many Brookings staff members continued to perform services for New Deal agencies. Henry Seidemann, a long-time staff member, worked out measures for the payment of agricultural benefits under the AAA and set up the Social Security Administration's vast system of accounting for payroll taxes and benefits. Isador Lubin was appointed commissioner of labor statistics at a time when the federal government was seeking to improve its data-gathering and statistical dissemination. Leo Pasvolsky went to the State Department, setting up a research operation that foreshadowed the more formal Policy Planning Staff, instituted after World War II. Even Leverett Lyon, exceedingly skeptical of the NRA, served for a time in that agency before returning to Brookings to pursue further research on the recovery program and head the training division. By the late 1930s some sixty-five former staff members or students were at work in New Deal agencies.

Direct service to government—advising and consulting, scrutinizing agencies and programs—was only part of the role Brookings played in the 1930s. The economists embarked on a large-scale study to understand the underlying causes of the depression. With financial support from the Maurice and Laura Falk Foundation of Pittsburgh, they explored national income levels, patterns of consumption and investment, and the productive capacities of the American economy. The four volumes of the so-called Capacity series, published between 1933 and 1935, were the most ambitious early effort to gain an empirical understanding of, and to chart a way out of, the depression.[5] The series (the first two volumes sold about 10,000 copies each, while the last had a distribution of over 100,000 copies through the Falk Foundation) greatly influenced contemporary insights into the causes of the economic crisis. Walter Lippmann described it as "the most useful economic study made in America during the depression."

In analyzing capital formation, the Brookings researchers argued that Americans had been unable to accumulate significant savings during the 1920s. Their analysis of American production concluded that the economy's productive capacities were poorly utilized even in the years of prosperity during the 1920s. They attributed the failure to the reluctance of producers to reduce prices as costs fell; the result was a maldistribution of both wage gains and profits. Following lines of institutional economic analysis suggested in Thorstein Veblen's work at the turn of the century, the Brookings researchers faulted several decades of corporate consolidation and the growth of trusts, cartels, trade associations, and the "codes" sanctioned by the National Industrial Recovery Act. They concluded that income would have to be more equitably distributed if the economy were ever to function smoothly. The studies, eerily resonant nearly sixty years later, were especially critical of the concentrations of capital that had been diverted from productive investment and toward speculation and industrial mergers during the 1920s. Far from expounding a radical redistributionist argument, however, the studies were in keeping with the most conservative traditions of scientific management. The Brookings volumes contended that if business firms could be made more efficient, prices could be lowered, real wages would consequently rise, and living standards would improve for everyone.

At the heart of the argument was the efficiency expert's conviction that employer and employee had mutual interests that could be harmonized through more efficient and economical industrial operations. "The highway along which continued economic progress must be sought is the avenue of price reductions. When this road is followed the benefits of technical improvements are conferred automatically upon the divisions of the population."[6] Stuart Chase, the prolific popularizer of liberal economic ideas, found the overall analysis persuasive, but faulted Brookings for falling short in its policy recommendations. Brookings "throws up its hands and goes to sleep on the broad bosom of old mother laissez-faire. Lower prices secured by free competition is [its] solution."[7] Chase concluded that direct redistribution through the tax system or transfer programs had more to offer; in contrast, Moulton and his colleagues placed their faith in the efficiency of the business corporation and the market rather than in the powers of government, though their analysis showed how modern business enterprises had created institutional structures to prevent the market's pricing mechanisms from working correctly.

From 1936 onward Brookings found itself more and more often in the same camp as the conservative opponents of the New Deal, arguing against the growing concentrations of power in the executive branch, denouncing federal interventions in the economy, and viewing public works and welfare programs as little more than schemes for buying votes. Roosevelt's plans to reorganize the executive office pushed Brookings into even more vehement opposition. In 1937 Frederic Delano, troubled by the widening gulf between Brookings researchers and his nephew's administration, resigned from the board. Moulton asserted that the institution's criticism had never been grounded in partisanship, although during the 1930s the board added several highly vocal critics of the New Deal.

The role of Brookings in Washington was clearly undergoing changes. For one thing, economists rather than public administrators were now charting the intellectual direction for the institution. Rather than serving as administrative consultants to government agencies as they implemented policies, Brookings scholars were looking critically at the impact of government programs on the economy. Moreover, the old intellectual distinction between politics and administration—the gospel of the first-generation public administration scholars—seemed increasingly untenable as the federal government assumed wider social and economic responsibilities. Government's wartime expansion and the embrace of Keynesian-inspired fiscal tools would drive Brookings further into opposition.

War Work and an Era's End

If economists and policymakers were divided in their efforts to understand the depression and find a way out of it during the 1930s, they proved much more adept during the 1940s at orchestrating the wartime economic mobilization and preparing for peace. One economist, noting the celebrated military role of chemists in World War I and physicists in World War II, argued that World War II might legitimately be termed the "economists' war." Certainly economists ended the war with a far stronger claim than other social scientists that they alone had the intellectual tools for helping political leaders frame their policy choices.

With the outbreak of World War II, however, Brookings researchers turned to discrete and urgent topics. Studies of military manpower needs helped Congress balance the requirements of the armed services against the demand for civilian labor in a war economy; other studies dealt with wartime pricing policies, rationing schemes, and nondefense budget cuts. Brookings staff members built on their studies of the economy's productive capacities with reports for a variety of governmental agencies; they examined steel, aluminum, and automobile production as well as the nation's electrical power capacity.

Brookings made itself especially useful to Congress, helping with various bills, including war labor measures and tax changes. The

National Resources Planning Board was aiding the executive branch in postwar planning, so Congress turned primarily to Brookings to counter the research of the liberal Keynesians at the NRPB. Brookings work for Senator Walter George's Special Senate Committee on Post-War Economic Policy and Planning helped speed the end of wartime economic controls and stave off expansive postwar New Deal social measures. A study of the postwar administration of Germany and Japan, thanks to the Book-of-the-Month Club, received wider distribution than any Brookings publication before or since.

Gradually, the Brookings resident staff shrank to only a handful of old-timers as the younger scholars went into the military or other wartime agencies. With so few remaining staff members, the two research divisions (last vestiges of the original institutes) were consolidated and the programs of the training division suspended. Foundation grants, which by the late 1930s had climbed considerably from the depths of the early 1930s, fell off again during the war. However, the reduced staff and program, combined with Moulton's shrewd investment policies, meant that endowment income could meet half the institution's expenses. There was leeway to plan, and Moulton and his colleagues looked ahead to the institution's postwar research program.

Moulton, far and away the dominant voice among the Brookings economists, and always a vigorous polemicist, hewed to a conservative course as the domestic research program took shape in the mid-1940s. He deplored the new policy consensus, grounded in Keynesian ideas, that was forming as the war came to an end. Economists, thanks to the Employment Act of 1946, which among other things set up the Council of Economic Advisers, assumed a powerful voice (including a formal advisory role) in national policymaking. Even though the Council was initially chaired by Brookings vice president Edwin Nourse, Moulton and the institution swam against the intellectual currents of their academic discipline. Moulton turned the institution into an outpost of anti-Keynesianism, denouncing what he called the "new economics" and the "new philosophy of public debt."

He attacked one of the key assumptions of Keynes's American disciples, namely, that the economy had reached a state of maturity and would stagnate without systematic public investment and deficit spending. In many respects, he was a better student of economic history, technology, and institutions than his Keynesian opponents, who were convinced that the economy suffered from what they called "secular stagnation." Moulton believed that technological changes drove the economy, and he saw rich opportunities for private capital investment if only the system of private enterprise could be protected from government controls and the distortions caused by excessive public spending. His belief that public spending would inevitably lead to inflation, and that the attempts to control inflation would in turn result in calls for tighter economic control, led him to predict dangerous consequences: "With unlimited debt expansion we cannot prevent inflation without the use of totalitarian methods of control. No compromise or half-way measures can adjust the difficulties. The choice is between regimentation and inflation."[8]

His combative style, and by some accounts his willful distortions of Keynesian ideas, left Brookings isolated. Some economists felt they could not work freely under Moulton's strong hand. Recruitment of new staff to replace the veterans who had arrived in the 1920s proved difficult. Moreover, the end of the training program further isolated Brookings from the theoretical work under way in university economics departments. Meanwhile, foundation staff members, listening to the advice of academic economists, grew increasingly reluctant to support the now dated Brookings work in institutional economics.

The economic research program at Brookings took on a predictable quality as it opposed virtually every domestic initiative of the Truman administration. The extension of social security and unemployment insurance, new provisions for the disabled, and plans for compulsory health insurance were all criticized on the ground that they threatened to sap the nation's economic vitality. "The desire for security," Moulton warned, "has become so compelling that increasing numbers of people appear to treasure security above freedom and self-reliance."[9] Unless the growth of federal social programs were checked, Moulton predicted a vast expansion and politicization of the federal bureaucracy. Unlike the founders of the Institute for Government Research, Moulton feared that bureaucracy would be a tool of partisan and special interests. His analysis returned to the harmful potential of deficit spending. A large bureaucracy administering federal programs and undisciplined by the need to balance the federal budget seemed to Moulton to possess a frightening mechanism for retaining an indefinite hold on political power.

In 1950, two years from retirement, Moulton proudly, and revealingly, recalled what he viewed as the institution's most noteworthy recent achievement: a record of legislation undone, altered, or stopped. Brookings had helped speed the end of wartime economic controls. It had worked to moderate the proposed Full Employment Bill by preventing measures to guarantee jobs through public works expenditures. Thanks to Lewis Meriam's work, Brookings had played its part in halting national health insurance. Harold Metz's work on federal labor policy helped the proponents of the Taft-Hartley Act undo provisions of the earlier Wagner Act.

International Studies

While the Brookings approach to domestic social and economic policy represented a rear-guard defense, its International Studies group under Leo Pasvolsky proved much more innovative. Pasvolsky, who earlier had earned his Ph.D. from the Brookings Graduate School, was one of the key researchers involved in Brookings studies of war debts and reparations during the 1920s. He and Moulton turned out studies of Germany, France, the Soviet Union, and Japan in the interwar years. Throughout the 1930s they argued for mechanisms to expand world trade and ease international foreign exchange problems. They correctly saw the catastrophic political consequences of mishandling debts, reparations, and reconstruction when vindictive national policies savaged the framework of international trade and finance. With a vision for building global free markets, the institution lobbied throughout the 1930s for foundation support for an expanded international program, but to no avail until the war forcefully propelled the United States into a wider international role.

Pasvolsky, who served at the State Department from 1935 to 1946 while maintaining close ties to Brookings, coordinated research on postwar foreign policy and was involved in the planning that led to the creation of the International Monetary Fund, the International Bank for Reconstruction and Development, and the United Nations. When he returned to Brookings, he assembled a group of researchers drawn from among those officials he had worked with in government. Funded largely by the Rockefeller Foundation, the International Studies group defined several goals. In the short term, they felt that as outsiders who had served in government they had expert advice to offer those people who still served in government. Over the long term, they aimed to create a body of well-trained experts in international affairs and to shape a more enlightened public opinion. They understood that American policies were several steps ahead of the public's traditionally isolationist sentiments.

Seasoned by their government service, they brought to their studies at Brookings a "problem" approach, which they sometimes likened to a business school's case method. Their approach yielded many publications, notably annual surveys of American foreign policy problems, monthly reports on specific issues, and a pamphlet series. They were widely used in new college and university courses when academic programs in international affairs were just getting off the ground. Indeed, the Brookings International Studies group through its publications and seminars tried to steer the budding international affairs programs in American universities in practical, problem-oriented directions. In the end, Brookings helped strengthen the rival university-based training and research programs.

Pasvolsky and his staff continued to serve policymakers directly. They stepped in when Senator Arthur Vandenberg, chairman of the Senate Foreign Relations Committee, asked the Brookings scholars to help devise an administrative structure for the European Recovery Program, as the Marshall Plan was formally known. Brookings, by recommending an organizational scheme, reassured those who were wary of a give-away program that the plan would be run carefully and on a businesslike basis. Work on the Marshall Plan underscored the two dominant concerns of the International Studies group: the organization and implementation of foreign policy and foreign assistance programs and their administration. Before his death in 1953 Pasvolsky also set in motion a series of studies of the United Nations, which yielded important volumes throughout the 1950s.

But the International Studies program was not without its critics. Its practical orientation did not win universal admiration among academic specialists in foreign affairs. In the late 1940s and early 1950s, the institution could not shake a growing sense among foundation executives and academics that its work was not up to the highest university standards. There were complaints about the caliber of the staff, some of whom had been with the institution since the early 1920s and whose most productive days were at an end. The predictable polemical tone of some publications also troubled academic observers. Jerome Greene, present at the creation of the Institute for Government Research and a long-time Brookings board member, worriedly told a friend at the Rockefeller Foundation, "These criticisms are coming not from the ones whose political views make them not like the conclusions of Brookings studies, but from scientists and scholars who do not respect the quality of the work, the quality of the personnel which is being appointed and the degree of centralization of power in President Moulton's hands."[10]

To his credit, Moulton had ensured the institution's survival through two difficult decades. Its endowment had risen to $6.6 million (from $2.3 million in 1928) and its annual budget was well over $800,000 (a substantial increase from budgets in the 1920s and 1930s that had been in the $300,000 range). Its research, though it had increasingly antagonized liberal groups, had left a mark on policy discussions. Over the years, officials of the executive branch and members of Congress had found that Brookings could be counted on for timely data, an administrative report, or legislative advice. As Moulton approached retirement, however, questions about the research program and even about prospects for the institution's long-term survival complicated the search for a successor. Any successor would face the difficult assignment of revitalizing the staff, reorganizing the research program, and regaining the confidence of foundation supporters and the academic community.

3

A THINK TANK
COMES OF AGE

ROBERT D. CALKINS was first approached about the Brookings presidency in 1948, while Harold Moulton was still several years from retirement. Calkins, a Virginian from Williamsburg, had been trained in economics at Stanford University and was at the crest of a remarkably successful career as an academic administrator. He had been named chairman of the economics department at the University of California, Berkeley, while still an assistant professor, and had risen to become dean of its College of Commerce. He subsequently went to New York as dean of Columbia University's School of Business and moved into Rockefeller philanthropic circles in the 1940s. In 1947 he was named vice president and director of the Rockefeller-funded General Education Board.

When the subject of the Brookings post was first raised, however, he demurred, saying that he was not ready to give up his foundation position after only a year on the job. His reluctance was reinforced, no doubt, when friends in the foundation community warned him that prospects for the Brookings Institution's survival looked very bleak. Nevertheless, the Brookings board continued to see him as an ideal successor to Moulton, and in 1952 he finally accepted the institution's presidency.

Rebuilding Brookings

Calkins brought valuable qualities to the job. He was well regarded in philanthropic circles, a friend and protégé of Raymond B. Fosdick, long-time Rockefeller Foundation president and a member of the Brookings board from 1916 to 1931 (and an honorary member from 1966 to 1972). By nature a conciliatory and personable man, he was admired as an experienced academic administrator (he had also worked as a labor negotiator) and seemed to share not only Robert Brookings's vision for the institution but his instincts as a builder. In the view of senior fellow Henry J. Aaron, Calkins's contributions to Brookings during his fifteen-year tenure as president have been "much under-praised." "He built the building, he raised the endowment, and he hired Joe Pechman, not necessarily in that order of importance," observed Aaron.

Calkins faced several tasks upon his arrival. Nearly forty years later, he reflected that the principal need was to develop greater academic prestige for the policy research enterprise. "I had had a feeling even in the 1920s that a lot of my colleagues were contemptuous of those who wrote on policy questions. Most in the academic community believed in the value of fundamental research, not applied research," he recalled. There were many more professional perquisites and intellectual rewards for social scientists working in university settings than in a Washington-based applied research institute. Calkins was justifiably worried about recruiting a high-quality research staff and knew that the institution's reputation in foundation circles might hinder his efforts to rebuild.

His first steps in 1952 were to cut the staff sharply, from about 120 to 60 (only 8 of Moulton's 20 senior fellows remained). He then looked to the nation's universities for some first-rate economists around whom the research program could be reorganized. The competition with the universities was tough, and the institution's reputation as "Moulton's establishment" seemed to linger well into the late 1950s.

Calkins persisted in trying to attract first-rate academics to Brookings, convinced that unless the institution "produces research that commands the respect of the scholarly community, it has nothing to offer the public."[1] He felt, too, that the program had become fragmented, dealing with targets of opportunity and responding to the availability of project financing rather than trying to build a series of intellectually related studies.

Consulting with an outside academic advisory group and foundation executives, he gradually reshaped the research staff and program. Walter Salant was the sort of economist Calkins wanted, a man with extensive government experience and outstanding academic credentials. Hired by Calkins in 1954, Salant had been a student of both John Maynard Keynes at Cambridge and Alvin Hansen, among others, at Harvard. He had put his professional training to work in Washington at the Office of Price Administration and as economic adviser to the economic stabilization director during the war and had served in the Commerce Department and on the staff of the Council of Economic Advisers afterward. His Keynesian training and work within the government's new array of economic advisory institutions set him apart from most of Moulton's economists.

Calkins further strengthened relations between Brookings and the academic community by renewing the fellowship program in 1955 with the aim of bringing graduate students to Brookings for a year of study. In 1955 he also reorganized Brookings into its three present-day research divisions—Economic Studies, Governmental Studies, and Foreign Policy Studies. The old foundation supporters signaled their approval with new grants, while a close relationship was forged with the Ford Foundation, which had emerged from regional obscurity in 1950 to become the nation's largest private foundation and an important funder of social science research.

New programs took shape in each of the three divisions, but the studies did not break completely with the past. A. D. H. Kaplan had begun to look at big business in the 1940s, publishing *Big Enterprise in a Competitive System* in 1954. The economists continued to look at transportation policy. Wilfred Owen's *The Metropolitan Transportation Problem*, published in 1956, was a highly regarded volume. Calkins expanded the institution's work in international economics and began to explore the fields of government finance and economic growth and stabilization policy.

Several research projects begun in the late 1950s would stand out as significant Brookings contributions to the discipline of economics, providing evidence of the institution's scholarly maturation. John G. Gurley and Edward S. Shaw's *Money in a Theory of Finance* (1961) began as an institutional study of trends in commercial banking. It gradually evolved into a book that broke new theoretical ground by studying money and finance not as problems of historical and institutional description—as they had traditionally been studied—but as market problems. Gurley and Shaw asked questions about the supply and demand for financial assets and sought to distinguish the various markets for financial assets. The book thus began to link financial markets to other markets and to provide a theoretical basis for understanding the role that money plays in economic growth and equilibrium. The increasing technical sophistication of Brookings work was also apparent in Walter Salant and Beatrice N. Vaccara's *Import Liberalization and Employment* (1961), which was a pioneering application of Wassily Leontieff's input-output analysis. Their work employed new methods to explore the effects on employment of relaxing international trade barriers.

The Governmental Studies scholars began gradually to shift away from narrowly defined questions about public administration to study politics and political processes. With Paul T. David heading the Governmental Studies program, the institution (in collaboration with the American Political Science Association) examined the presidential nominating process. Their research effort led to a series of studies of presidential selection, the electoral process, and presidential transitions.

After Pasvolsky's death in 1953 some staff members expressed doubts about continuing the international program, but Calkins remained committed to its work, much of it focusing on the United Nations. Robert Hartley, who succeeded Pasvolsky, supervised the studies, hiring outside scholars and opening a New York office. The United Nations project included studies by Leland Goodrich and Anne Simons on the maintenance of international peace, Francis Wilcox and Carl Marcy on proposed changes in the UN structure and operations, James Greer on human rights, Emil Sady on dependent peoples, Robert Asher and colleagues on economic and social cooperation, and Ruth Russell on the UN charter. They were generally well reviewed and highly regarded as historical and institutional studies, but they did not focus on topics that were matters of great urgency to the Eisenhower administration. Even if the timing and political context for some of the Brookings work was not yet ripe, Calkins's hiring and research plans were nonetheless beginning to yield results.

In 1957 the institution faced an entirely unforeseen threat to its existence. The federal government wanted to construct a new office building near the White House. Its plans encompassed the Jackson Place site that Brookings had inhabited since 1931. Suddenly the institution was faced with finding a new home—and given only three years to relocate or build new headquarters. It was an opportunity for the institution to revisit questions its board and staff had not systematically contemplated since the late 1920s. What kind of role should such an institution play in the nation's public policy process?

Where should it physically situate itself in Washington? What new facilities would be required to support a research program and to have Brookings play a greater role as an educational institution?

Calkins devised ambitious plans—to build a new facility three times larger than the old building. The project would require $9 million in capital funds and sufficient money to double the annual operating budget, then at a level of approximately $1 million. Various new sites were considered and discarded. "We simply couldn't go north of Massachusetts Avenue," he decided, and a parcel of land was pieced together near Dupont Circle. Foundations, typically reluctant to put their resources into "brick and mortar" grants, resisted for a time. After spending considerable time in New York, including two day-long sessions at the Ford Foundation, where "they put us on the grill," Calkins won enough financing for construction to begin. The key backer, in fact, was the Ford Foundation, which in 1958 gave most of the money for the planned expansion. It was the largest sum that Brookings had ever received, $5 million in operating support over ten years and $1.2 million for the building's construction (overcoming its initial reluctance, the Rockefeller Foundation gave $500,000 toward construction of an annex to the main building, where other nonprofit groups would be housed).

Although Ford had given an earlier general support grant of $1 million, this new commitment marked the beginning of a relationship between Ford and Brookings that would yield nearly $25 million of Ford money for Brookings in the period from 1955 to 1964. In some years, more than one-third of Brookings annual budget was derived from Ford grants. The foundation staff members were convinced that Brookings could become "a major national asset in the form of a private intelligence unit for government operations, the source of a stream of suggestions for national policy based on objective research."[2] For Calkins, Brookings stood on the threshold of becoming the one major national institution capable of systematically looking at emerging policy issues and marshaling the nation's intellectual resources to study public policy questions. Indeed, the new facility was to be called the Center for Advanced Study, the name itself implying a more scholarly role for Brookings and suggesting stronger relationships with the growing numbers of university-based policy scholars and their students.

Experts on Tap

The opening of the new Brookings building in November 1960 was timely. Not only did its dedication coincide with a national election and the enthusiasms that typically surround a presidential transition, but its opening came when government and academic social scientists seemed increasingly receptive to collaboration. New models for such collaboration were taking shape. In fact, the term "think tank" (borrowed from World War II military jargon) first entered wide popular usage in the 1960s to describe such institutions. The popularity of the term was a sign of the growing prominence of expert advisers working in institutions that were not altogether familiar.

In the early 1960s Brookings and the Rand Corporation, though very different as organizational types and in their respective research programs, were the institutions that embodied the image of the modern think tank. They typified the era's fascination with expertise and technical know-how. Yet the very amorphousness of the term also suggests how diverse the various institutional experiments with research and advising have been.

With the opening of the new Brookings research center, observers in Washington's press corps saw great promise in the nation's "brain banks" and "think factories." A *Time* magazine writer strained for meaningful historical analogies, saying that Brookings "aims to create Washington's first real Delphi—a place for probing the hidden patterns of modern society and assuring the 'intellectual preparedness' of key

Americans." Meanwhile, the *Economist* wrote about Brookings as a place with "experts on tap" for government, while the *Wall Street Journal* saw it as a "researcher, teacher for Uncle Sam." Certainly, the links to policymakers were becoming more apparent by the early 1960s, although the precise impact of research on particular decisions was no more clear-cut than it had ever been.

Almost as soon as Brookings opened its new building, it found itself involved in the the 1960 presidential transition. Today, many of Washington's most industrious think tanks routinely focus their energies on producing voluminous policy briefing books to be released in election years as handbooks for candidates and other aspiring officeholders; some even participate in the presidential appointments competition, collecting and circulating the résumés of prospective appointees.

Brookings studies of presidential nominations and elections in the 1950s had led to a study of transitions and the publication of Laurin Henry's *Presidential Transitions* early in 1960. His book provided the framework for a series of papers prepared in consultation with both the Kennedy and Nixon camps that were designed to smooth the way for the victor in setting up a new administration. The confidential papers—quite different from the public agendas and well-promoted policy pronouncements now emanating from think tanks each election year—dealt with both issues and administrative decisions. They opened the door for Brookings scholars to participate in some of the early planning groups and task forces assembled by the Kennedy administration.

The presidential transition project suggests how relatively easy communications across the divide between government and the private research sector have typically been in the United States. Rather than relying on a permanent governmental bureaucracy, elected officials turn more readily to private research institutions for research and advice. These exceedingly fluid relationships permit people and ideas to pass relatively easily among government agencies, private research

Born in 1850, Robert S. Brookings worked as a traveling salesman for a St. Louis woodenware firm, Cupples and Marston, in his teens and twenties. In his forties he retired to pursue philanthropic interests.

Brookings moved to Washington during World War I and spent the last decade of his life building the institution that came to bear his name.

Brookings worked with Andrew Carnegie in various philanthropic endeavors, and the Carnegie Corporation was the primary supporter of the Institute of Economics. Here they are pictured at Chamonix, France, in 1913.

In his sixties Brookings served on the War Industries Board, the principal body for coordinating economic policy during World War I. Among his colleagues was Bernard Baruch, seated second from left.

In 1927 Brookings married Isabelle Vallé January, a long-time friend and daughter of a St. Louis businessman. She was an early supporter of the Brookings Graduate School and continued to be a major benefactor of the institution after her husband's death.

Jerome D. Greene, secretary of the Rockefeller Foundation, was one of the prime movers behind the Institute for Government Research, Washington's oldest policy research center. He drafted its first prospectus in 1915.

Staff members from the Brookings Institution's early years gathered in 1952 for a retirement party. They included Lewis Meriam, Leverett Lyon, William Willoughby, and Edwin Nourse.

The Robert S. Brookings Graduate School opened in 1924. During its four-year existence it was attended by 120 students and awarded 74 doctorates. Here graduates in 1928 pose for a photograph.

After service in the State Department, Leo Pasvolsky, a graduate of the Brookings Graduate School, returned to Brookings in 1946 and set up the International Studies group, which he directed until 1953.

Harold G. Moulton was named director of the Institute of Economics in 1922. He became president of the Brookings Institution after its merger in 1927 and served until 1952.

The Brookings Institution occupied a building at 722 Jackson Place, a stone's throw from the White House, from 1932 until 1960.

Since 1960 the Brookings Institution has been located at 1775 Massachusetts Avenue, one block from Dupont Circle.

Robert D. Calkins, an economist who taught at the University of California, Berkeley, and Columbia University, served as president of Brookings from 1952 to 1967.

Speaking at the Brookings Institution's fiftieth anniversary, Lyndon B. Johnson, pictured with Robert Calkins, sought to repair shaky relationships with the nation's intellectuals.

institutions, foundations, and universities. However, the easy interchange does not mean that policy research and academic expertise alone can determine the final outcome of policy deliberations.

In the 1960s Brookings was called upon to undertake research projects for the Council of Economic Advisers, the State Department, the Agency for International Development, and other government units; it collaborated with universities, research bodies such as Rand, the National Bureau of Economic Research, and the Institute for Defense Analysis. Through much of the decade, as many as one hundred research projects were under way at any given moment. Even though the sheer volume of work might suggest a diffuse intellectual program, much of the work was concentrated in only a few areas. Two areas—government finance and transportation—accounted for about one-third of the research projects.

The Government Finance program, which in its first phase from 1960 to 1967 was funded by the Ford Foundation, was a large national undertaking directed by Joseph A. Pechman. Pechman, who directed the Brookings Economic Studies program from 1962 to 1983, not only shaped an exemplary research effort on tax policy but set the pattern for research in other policy areas. Educated at the City College of New York and trained in economics at the University of Wisconsin, he served briefly in a junior capacity in the Office of Price Administration during the early stages of World War II and later worked on the staffs of the Treasury Department and the Council of Economic Advisers. After four years with the Committee for Economic Development, he joined Brookings in 1960. In his thirty-year association with Brookings, he showed an uncanny knack for recruiting high-quality staff and lent his unique intellectual excitement, warmth, and high spirit to the program.

The Government Finance program aimed ambitiously to measure the economic impact of various taxes, to develop criteria for evaluating the efficiency of government expenditures, to explore questions of tax equity, and to look for ways to reduce tax rates, lessen the complexity of the tax laws, and increase voluntary compliance. The program involved institutional collaboration with universities and other research groups and involved well over one hundred scholars when it was in full swing. Its work ranged across state and local government and touched on virtually every source of government revenue, yielding some twenty-five books and fifty doctoral dissertations through its first phase; another thirty books were published before Pechman's death in 1989.

Among the major early volumes were Wilfred Lewis, Jr.'s *Federal Fiscal Policy in Postwar Recessions* (1962) and Richard Goode's *The Individual Income Tax* (1964). Lewis's volume was the first of the long series; it analyzed each of the four postwar recessions, showing that automatic fiscal stabilizers in each instance slowed the economic decline. After interviewing the principal economic policymakers in each administration, he concluded that government officials were becoming much more skillful in using fiscal policy tools. He looked at the impact of those tools as well, finding that the automatic stabilizers that affected personal income (the income tax, unemployment compensation, and employment taxes) had cushioned personal income declines and tempered the impact of postwar recessions. Discretionary actions, Lewis found, had proved much less helpful in responding to recessions.

Goode, appraising the income tax fifty years after the legislation was drafted, chronicled its transformation from a tax covering only 1 percent of the population to a mass tax covering about 75 percent of Americans and yielding nearly half of all federal revenues. Moreover, the income tax had become a primary instrument of federal intervention in the economy. Goode found the income tax better than any other tax in aligning the tax burden with ability to pay and in tempering income inequalities. But he also saw serious defects that had crept in over the years, narrowing the tax base and creating structural inequities. His various proposals—expanding the tax base by redefining taxable income, treating capital gains less preferentially, and creating an earned income credit—anticipated most of the past quarter century's debates over the income tax. Goode foresaw the difficulties of enacting sweeping tax legislation and urged patient piecemeal improvements.

The program of research on government finance yielded dozens of technical studies analyzing the economic consequences of particular taxes, exploring individual economic behavior, and looking at finance and budgeting at the state and local levels. Among the many volumes, three stand out for dissipating the fog that has often enveloped debates about budgets and tax policy. David J. Ott and Attiat F. Ott wrote *Federal Budget Policy* (1965), an introduction to the subject for the general reader that sought especially to explain the uses of federal spending as an instrument of economic policy. James A. Maxwell wrote *Financing State and Local Governments* (1965) to introduce citizens to taxing and spending at those levels of government that account for most of the nation's spending on education, roads, welfare, public health, and sanitation. His study appraised the health of American federalism and was one of the first to explore the nature of the grant system for transferring national revenues to states and localities. Maxwell saw urgent problems with state and local reliance on property and sales taxes. He called for a "cooperative federalism," which would allow states and localities to handle problems more directly, thus forestalling greater centralization of governmental power. Joseph A. Pechman's *Federal Tax Policy* (1966) dealt with such quandaries as the relationship between taxes and economic growth, and tax policy and the legislative process. Pechman explored the various tax options—personal income tax, corporate income tax, consumption taxes, estate and gift taxes— summarizing much of the work of the government finance program. Pechman's volume assessed the strengths and weaknesses of the tax system, pointing toward reforms that would make it both more equitable and a better instrument for maintaining a strong economy.

Over the course of twenty years, the studies undertaken by Pechman and his colleagues provided the intellectual rationale for a tax system that would rely on a broad base of taxable income with lower rates and many fewer loopholes. Through scores of books, articles, conferences, seminars, informal consultation, congressional testimony, and the gradual process of educating editorial writers and journalists, Pechman and his colleagues pushed toward the consensus that finally bore fruit in the tax reform legislation of 1986. The lines of intellectual influence are certainly not direct and cannot be simply diagrammed, but over the years their arguments and evidence proved persuasive in the policy process.

The other large-scale research effort of the 1960s, the Transport Research program under Wilfred Owen, was established in 1962 with nearly $1.5 million from the Agency for International Development. It focused on the role of transportation in developing nations. As recently as the 1960s, in two-thirds of the world much of the trade moved by rickshaw, bullock cart, camel, or mule; animal muscle power set sharp limits to the pace of economic and social development. Yet in that decade new transportation systems were being planned, with some countries devoting as much as 40 percent of their development funds to large-scale projects. The impact of transport on development was uncharted territory—some projects opened new markets and brought prosperity, others proved wasteful and foolish. Scholars were enlisted from around the country, and the transportation research led to case studies of Latin American, Asian, and African transport. Scholars looked in a broad way at investment difficulties in regions where there were severe capital shortages, and they investigated transport maintenance problems in locales where environmental conditions were sometimes severe. The project's initial volume, Wilfred Owen's *Strategy for Mobility* (1964), offered a framework for developing countries to plan their transport needs, choose among alternative systems, decide how much to invest, and administer the construction and maintenance of a system. Owen urged planners to put transportation into a broader developmental context, seeing it not as a separate economic sector but as the interconnecting fiber for the whole economy.

The research at Brookings does not propel policy in entirely new directions. It can, however, redirect thinking through the analysis of a concept, the introduction of a new line of analysis, the assessment of alternatives, or the projection of the consequences of pursuing a particular policy. In the mid-1960s the institution undertook a study of the U.S. balance of payments at the request of the Council of Economic Advisers (CEA), the Treasury Department, and the Bureau of the Budget. Walter Salant directed a team of scholars that looked several years ahead at the balance of payments, linking their projections to policy advice that challenged conventional thinking about trade policy regarding international payments. Estimating the "basic" balance of payments (the U.S. net payments position on account of goods and services, long-term capital, and foreign aid) six years ahead, they argued on the basis of assumptions about the U.S. economy supplied by the CEA that the deficit in the U.S. basic balance would be inconsequential by the late 1960s.

The report looked at the complex interrelationships that determine the balance of payments, suggesting that any balance is largely a reflection of internal developments in the economies of the United States and its trading partners. Moreover, the Brookings scholars argued that there was not a one-to-one relationship between the balance of payments and the dollar's weakness in the early 1960s and that drastic efforts to reduce the U.S. deficit would create serious economic problems for other industrial nations. An obsessive preoccupation with trade deficits threatened more significant national economic objectives, the Brookings scholars warned. What was needed instead was a system with sufficient liquidity to permit nations to adjust gradually in times of deficit. Within two months of the study's publication in August 1963, Robert Calkins concluded that it had provoked more policy discussion than any previous Brookings study. In short order, it had shifted the focus of policy debate from talk of closing the deficit to plans for changing the international monetary system in order to improve liquidity.

While the policy implications of the economists' analytical work were often obvious (although the impact was rarely so clear-cut as in the balance-of-payments study), the Governmental Studies program tended to produce studies of less direct policy significance. The political scientists over the years have been students of process and observers of political dynamics. In the 1960s the long-standing administrative concerns of Brookings scholars were still in evidence as they looked at the conditions of government employment. Marver Bernstein's *The Job of the Federal Executive* (1958) had marked the beginning of a series of books that looked at public service. In the 1960s, research projects examined the attitudes of federal employees toward their work as well as the image of the public servant among the populace at large. In *The Congressman: His Work as He Sees It,* Charles L. Clapp summarized the frustrations senators and representatives felt about their work, though no simple solutions seemed likely to ease the demands on their time and intellect. *The Image of the Federal Service* (1964) was the first volume in a collaboration between social psychologist Franklin P. Kilpatrick and political scientists Milton C. Cummings, Jr., and M. Kent Jennings. Its aim was to discover what Americans thought about federal employment so that government service could be made more attractive to talented people. Out of their surveys came a stream of suggestions for making federal careers more appealing. Their work was bolstered by several other studies. David Stanley's book, *The Higher Civil Service: An Evaluation of Federal Personnel Practices* (1964), dealt with the professional and scientific work force of the federal government. Dean E. Mann with Jameson W. Doig published *The Assistant Secretaries: Problems and Processes of Appointment* (1965), looking at the one hundred or so officials who are in key policymaking positions in the departments and independent agencies.

In the various books on the jobs of federal officials, recommendations for career development and training programs and more fluid careers reinforced Brookings direct involvement in the education of senior government officials. An experimental conference program in the late 1950s had evolved by 1962 into the institution's Advanced Study program, which became a separate operating division. Its training programs provided a model for federal executive training programs in various federal departments and propelled state and local governments in similar directions.

The Governmental Studies program also looked at the points of intersection between bureaucratic and political processes. Joseph Harris in *Congressional Control of Administration* (1964), for example, asked how Congress handled its supervisory and regulatory role over the bureaucracy. Harris was critical of the appropriations process for getting bogged down in excessive detail when looking at agency budgets. It neglected to take a broader perspective on the federal budget. He proposed a joint legislative-executive committee to examine the methods and aims of legislative oversight.

The Foreign Policy Studies program was the least developed of the three research divisions during the early 1960s. But some of its work proved innovative. Considerable energy—though few publications emerged—was devoted to a collaborative project involving eight research institutes in Latin America. It was designed to explore Latin American economic integration. Under the direction of Joseph Grunwald and Donald Baerresen, the project began to collect data on the economies of Latin America in 1964. Brookings research on the United Nations continued in the 1960s with studies of the UN's financial arrangements by John G. Stoessinger and its military operations in the Congo by Ernest W. Lefever.

By the early 1960s Robert Calkins had turned Brookings into the very model of the modern Washington think tank, transforming an institution shaped in the Progressive Era into an organization that could fit into the more complex postwar networks of policy expertise and advising. As he prepared to step down from the Brookings presidency in 1967, he left an institution much larger and more highly regarded than the one he had inherited in 1952. The number of research projects had increased fivefold to roughly one hundred; the books released each year had expanded from a half dozen to two dozen; the budget had increased from $800,000 a year to nearly $5 million; and the endowment had risen from $6.6 million to well over $30 million. The Advanced Study program was pursuing a robust series of public policy conferences and seminars that reached several thousand senior government officials, business executives, and professionals each year. A $20 million endowment campaign had also just been completed, with $10 million coming from the Ford Foundation and $8 million from the estate of Robert Brookings's widow. And nothing better symbolized the institution's secure presence in Washington than the stolid eight-story granite building near Dupont Circle, which Calkins had envisioned and built.

By the mid-1960s Brookings was at the center of a growing academic and policy network in Washington. It had no real rivals: the American Enterprise Institute was still a tiny operation, and the Santa Monica–based Rand Corporation had not yet turned to domestic policy research and did not have a significant presence in Washington. The Center for Strategic and International Studies and the Institute for Policy Studies were still fledgling organizations. The Urban Institute and Heritage Foundation had not yet been established. Calkins and his colleagues did not need to market their studies, to seek out opportunities to advise, to bid on research contracts, to promote specific policy ideas. Rather, they were sought out by government officials and worked quietly behind the scenes. The problems they confronted were often technical; the contributions they made did not often lend themselves to wide discussion for they were addressed to fellow professionals. As Calkins pointed out, "Our type of research does not create mass opinion to which leaders in government and private life respond." Rather, he explained, "It is sought and used by professional people in responsible positions who help shape public opinion and public policy." Over the long term, he felt, Brookings work would come to be reflected in "informed opinion."[3] And so it would be, as long as informed opinion was bounded by a broad consensus on the goals of economic and foreign policy. But with the unraveling of that consensus in the late 1960s, public policymaking could no longer be viewed as a matter requiring only technical skills and analytic virtuosity. Calkins's successors would have to confront a very different climate for serious policy research.

4

NEW AGENDAS

THE CHANGE OF LEADERSHIP at Brookings, befitting the institution that had studied presidential transitions, was a smooth one, completed in 1967 but effected over the course of two years. Kermit Gordon, third in the line of economists who have presided over Brookings, joined the staff as vice president in 1965. He took charge of the research program with the understanding that he would succeed Robert Calkins, who was then in his early sixties.

Gordon, born in Philadephia in 1916, received his undergraduate degree from Swarthmore in 1938. On the eve of World War II, he won a Rhodes scholarship and proceeded to University College, Oxford, where he was tutored by the future prime minister Harold Wilson. With the outbreak of war in Europe, he returned home to continue his graduate studies in economics at Harvard, but before completing his doctoral work, Gordon joined the young economists clustered at the Office of Price Administration in Washington. He moved on to the Office of Strategic Services during the last two years of the war.

After spending a year at the State Department, he accepted a teaching post at Williams College in 1946, where he taught for most of the next sixteen years. Two brief stints at the Ford Foundation (where he later served on the board) and work for the Merrill Foundation gave him a glimpse of the foundation world and its intersection with public policymaking.

Gordon was propelled to the center of national economic policymaking in 1961 when Walter Heller recruited him for service on President Kennedy's Council of Economic Advisers. After a year on the CEA, he was named budget director, a post that he retained under President Johnson. After three fast-paced years during which most of the Great Society legislation was set in place, Gordon was ready to leave government. In 1965 he turned down President Johnson's offer of the post of secretary of the treasury to join the Brookings Institution. For Gordon the post at Brookings was a chance to continue to play a role in the policy process but "from a less hectic and more contemplative vantage point" after four years of government service.[1]

When his colleagues describe Gordon, the adjective that often recurs is "elegant." Less a matter of personal style or bearing, the elegance characterized his thinking and speaking, a quality akin to the clarity and precision that mathematicians speak of when they describe an elegant proof. Although he wrote well and clearly, he published little during his academic career. Indeed, his exacting literary standards seem at times to have made it difficult for him to write—and sometimes even to edit the work of colleagues whose manuscripts were not up to the mark. "He valued the written word so highly," said one former colleague, "that the minute he ran across a poorly constructed sentence he said to himself it needs more work and he put the manuscript aside."

When Gordon arrived at Brookings from the Bureau of the Budget, he brought considerable confidence in the discipline of economics and the emerging field of policy analysis. "Modern fiscal analysis is in," he said. "It's accepted on a broad front." The 1964 tax cut had demonstrated the power of fiscal theory; and economists, who had won a formal place in government with the creation of the Council of Economic Advisers in 1946, were enjoying their success as macroeconomic advisers. Gordon's experience in the Budget Bureau had come at a time when economists were honing their skills as analysts of program and policy alternatives. "A day never passes when a systematic approach won't pay dividends," said Gordon of the economists' work at the Budget Bureau.[2] Convinced of the usefulness of analysis, he wanted Brookings to focus on more immediate policy problems, to analyze policy choices and their consequences, and to deal less with political processes and administrative concerns.

Like Calkins, Gordon saw Brookings as an institution primarily serving an audience of policy academics and governmental experts. Brookings, he thought, was "a bridge between the world of ideas and the world of action that will be used by intellectual intermediaries to improve public policy." Its role in shaping popular opinion and advising policymakers was indirect, low-key. Indeed, he was wary enough of publicity to occasionally caution Brookings scholars about writing for the popular media and to say emphatically that he would not seek popular reviews of Brookings books.[3]

His views on Brookings staff members' direct government service and on the institution's educational role were different from those of his predecessors. Moulton had produced popular, sometimes artfully done, summaries of Brookings research projects; he had experimented with using radio for disseminating ideas in the 1930s; and he had written for popular magazines. In contrast, Gordon viewed the Brookings book publishing operation as something comparable to a university press. Unlike Calkins, Gordon manifested little interest in the conferences and seminars organized by the Advanced Study program, apparently viewing them as marginal to the tasks of scholarly research and writing.

Although Gordon had held governmental posts in an era of liberal social reform, he was no less concerned about economy and efficiency in government than the institution's founding generation. Indeed, when Gordon wrote about economy, he invoked Edmund Burke, who had argued, "Economy is a distributive virtue, and consists not in saving but in selection. . . . Parsimony requires no providence, no sagacity, no powers of combination, no comparison, no judgment." He was critical of both conservatives and liberals, finding them confused about the meanings of economy. "If the confusion of parsimony with economy is the error that often entraps conservatives in their thinking about public budgets, there is a close symmetrical error that often appears on the liberal side. This is the confusion of profligacy with progress—the disposition to look with favor on an increase in total public spending just because it is an increase." In the end parsimony and profligacy were "false guides to policy for exactly the same reason: both deny the necessity for choice."[4]

Gordon's faith in social science, especially the discipline of economics, was rooted in the conviction that it offered tools for making intelligent choices. Setting priorities and analyzing trade-offs were the underlying themes of the Brookings program during Gordon's tenure. Whether policymakers had to confront "operating-level" questions or the "grand policy issues," in his words the institution's role was to provide an intellectual framework for assessing the options.[5]

The Nation's Changing Temper

Kermit Gordon assumed the presidency of Brookings in 1967 with a national election campaign not many months away. He saw an opening for a new project, building on earlier work by Brookings on the presidential transition. Gordon viewed national elections and transitions as moments to contemplate broad policy alternatives. "The nation has a sense that a page in history has been turned, and the new President has a blank sheet upon which to write," he observed.[6] Gordon planned to fill more than a few blank sheets of a large collaborative volume that would lay out priorities and choices for the nation in the 1970s.

A new U.S. president in 1969 would face the paramount objective of ending the fighting in Vietnam and confronting what Gordon termed the central paradox of American society: "On the one hand, we are a nation which sees itself as wracked and divided over problems of poverty, riots, race, slums, unemployment, and crime; on the other hand, we are a nation which is clearly enjoying high prosperity, rapid economic growth, and a steady diffusion of affluence at a rate almost unimaginable a decade ago."[7]

The paradox was not one to be resolved easily, as all Americans were soon to discover. The national doubts and confusions were scarcely amenable to research and reasoned discourse. Writing in 1968, Gordon felt that many of the nation's ills had been alleviated by a combination of economic prosperity and remedial public programs, though he was well aware that public perceptions of the extent of poverty and the impact of Great Society programs were already confused. The sources of perplexity and discontent were complex. But he was concerned that the gap between aspiration and performance had widened, arguing that the cause lay more in rising aspirations than in deteriorating government performance. Taking stock of the decade, he concluded that broad economic performance measured by gross national product and per capita disposable income had been a notable success. The nation's depressed areas, the "pockets of poverty" as they were characterized at the beginning of the 1960s, were much improved; many fewer families lived in poverty or in substandard housing; and he noted that many black Americans shared in some of the gains, although they still lagged far behind economically. Despite the gains in prosperity, some problems seemed to have worsened, especially crime, the decline of public education, and environmental pollution.

Agenda for the Nation, edited by Gordon, was the work of eighteen scholars (only three from Brookings). Arguing that prosperity alone was not enough, they found no panaceas for the nation's problems and were far more restrained than policy intellectuals writing at the beginning of the decade. Charles L. Schultze argued that a quick end to the fighting in Vietnam would yield no immediate solution to the government's financial problems; James L. Sundquist argued that private employment efforts would have to be supplemented by public employment and a national welfare policy if poverty were to be reduced more substantially; James Tobin urged the new administration to consider a negative income tax; and Kenneth B. Clark set out a sweeping plan for dealing with urban ghettos.

The essays on foreign policy were unified by general themes articulated in a chapter by Henry Kissinger, who argued that the age of the superpowers was ending and that a politically multipolar world was emerging. Military power, he felt, no longer could be translated into influence. The essays of both foreign and domestic analysts resonated with phrases such as turbulence, flux, complexity, paradox, and uncertainty. In taking the pulse of the nation in 1968, the authors were in a sense taking stock of expert knowledge at the end of a decade in which experts and intellectuals had come into their own as policy planners and advisers.

Some reviewers concluded harshly that the volume provided compelling evidence that the nation's intellectual stock was now depleted. One reviewer, who described the book as a project undertaken by "a sort of inner club of the American intellectual establishment," asked what it said about the establishment itself. While he found the establishment "darn good," he interpreted their musings as a sign of how "truly unhappy, almost despairing" they were. The nation's domestic problems, as described, seemed insoluble, agonizing, and terrifying; and the book, the collaborative work of some of the country's most distinguished policy scholars, was in the end "dispiriting."[8] The book, perhaps unwittingly, anticipated the policy temper of the 1970s. If the nation's own agenda were in so turbulent a state, what kind of research agenda could Brookings pursue to alleviate the national perplexity?

Government's Performance

Gordon had frequently commented on the widening gap between national aspirations and government performance in the late 1960s. He and his colleagues pursued the theme in the early 1970s. Gordon felt that the "doctrine of governmental incapacity" had undergone a revival. The sense that government programs were tainted by failure spanned the political spectrum. It was rooted less in recrudescent nineteenth-century ideologies (though those would revive soon enough in the 1970s) than in a widespread reaction to observed events. Too many costly programs had been set up too rapidly; their impact was less than promised. And even as they were being put in place, the nation felt itself torn apart by deepening crises of race, poverty, crime, and the environment. Gordon saw the problem primarily as a failure of analysis and planning. "Many [programs] were improvised in haste and on the foundation of the most perfunctory analysis. Most were thrown on the mercy of a federal adminstrative apparatus in which allied federal, state, and local officials rarely saw eye to eye either on strategy or tactics, and in which each group as often as not regarded the others as rivals and as impediments to progress."[9]

Acknowledging that there had been numerous recent failures, Gordon felt, nonetheless, that the sweeping indictment of government was vastly overdrawn. What he and his colleagues set out to do in the 1970s was to understand the recent record of both accomplishment and failure. Projects enlisting staff members in the Governmental Studies and Economic Studies programs explored the competence of government and sought to refine the intellectual tools available to those involved in planning, implementing, and evaluating policy. Large-scale study series were devoted to monitoring government performance, analyzing various social experiments, and exploring government regulation of economic activity. Brookings scholars also looked at the longer legacy of government activity, including social security, welfare, and work programs.

The new orientation of the Brookings program brought major changes in the Governmental Studies program. To reshape the program, Gordon chose Gilbert Y. Steiner, director of the Institute of Government and Public Affairs at the University of Illinois. Steiner had worked in the Illinois legislature and for the state government and had written books on social welfare policy, the U.S. Congress, and Illinois politics. To Steiner, the Brookings program of governmental research seemed rather dreary with its long-standing avoidance of politics and policy outcomes. But he was drawn to Washington as a vantage point for his continuing work on the politics of welfare policy and by Gordon's clear signal that he wanted the Governmental Studies program to change. "You worry about program and people, and I'll worry about money," he told Steiner.

As Steiner set out to reorient the Governmental Studies program he learned, as other program directors have, how different the staffing of an independent policy research institute is from a university social science department. Finding staff members with the ideal balance of scholarly detachment and practical government experience is always difficult. Moreover, in trying to attract senior scholars, Brookings must compete with the nation's most distinguished universities, whose financial resources are often greater and where inducements such as tenure (which senior faculty are customarily reluctant to give up) and the endless supply of talented research assistants are almost impossible to match.

Steiner thought it was particularly hard to recruit political scientists because so few of them had real government policymaking experience. He contrasted his problems with those of his colleagues in economics, complaining that "there are no 'natural' pools from which to recruit, like the Council of Economic Advisers." Kermit Gordon understood the difficulties. He estimated that fewer than one in ten of the former government officials who possessed the academic credentials to work at Brookings also had the temperament to produce books and scholarly studies, which, in the final analysis, is the paramount test of the Brookings scholar.

Given the innate obstacles, Steiner's recruitment paid off well in the late 1960s and early 1970s. He brought two prominent political scientists to Brookings. Herbert Kaufman was recruited from Yale University, where he had been chairman of the political science department, and Donald Matthews arrived from the University of North Carolina. He also brought in a younger group with political experience. He recruited Stephen Hess, who had served both presidents Eisenhower and Nixon. He brought back Richard Nathan, who had been at Brookings after working for Nelson Rockefeller and then had left for various policy assignments during Nixon's first term. And he lured to Washington a handful of promising young people who had not yet settled into tenure tracks at prestigious research universities, among them Martha Derthick from Boston College, Hugh Heclo from the Massachusetts Institute of Technology, Allen Schick from Tufts University, John Manley from the University of Wisconsin, Gary Orfield from Princeton University, and Chester Finn, a young academic on Daniel P. Moynihan's ambassadorial staff in India.

Already at Brookings was James Sundquist, who had come to the institution in 1965 after a career that spanned four years in journalism, a dozen in the civil service, five as an administrative assistant in the Senate, and brief stints with the Democratic National Committee and New York State government. His career in government was capped by service as deputy under secretary of agriculture. At Brookings he was at work on a study of politics and policymaking in the Eisenhower, Kennedy, and Johnson years, the first of six books he would write for Brookings during a twenty-year tenure.

Sundquist completed his study of policymaking from the Eisenhower to Johnson administrations in 1968. *Politics and Policy: The Eisenhower, Kennedy, and Johnson Years* was, in a sense, an antidote to growing complaints about the failure of the American political system. As key Brookings books sometimes do, it set the pattern for his colleagues' studies, exploring the institutional and political context in which policies were being made. He asked why American politics fluctuated between periods of inaction and spurts of initiative. What ingredients permitted some administrations to embark on significant policy changes? Were the conditions of change accidental—as some argued was the case in the Johnson legislative rush following the Kennedy assassination and landslide election of 1964—or were there systemic changes at work making the political system more responsive? He argued that the intellectual preparation for the programs of the mid-1960s was discernible in the 1950s. And as he examined the outpouring of legislation in 1964–65, following a decade of legislative deadlock, he argued that structural changes in Congress such as limitations on the power of the House Rules Committee and the curbing of Senate filibusters were making that body more responsive. Moreover, he predicted that a realignment of the parties was under way as the Republican party gained strength in the South. Parties more clearly identified as liberal and conservative would make it easier for the government to respond to the public will if, that is, the electorate clearly expressed its choice. It was a far more hopeful book, at least for the long term, than the almost contemporaneous *Agenda for the Nation*.

Sundquist continued his analysis of the underlying political transformation that many had discerned in the Republican electoral successes in 1968 and 1972. His *Dynamics of the Party System: Alignment and Realignment of Political Parties in the United States,* published in 1973, asked what conditions had brought about historic political realignments. Dominant issues—slavery in the 1850s, agrarian and labor unrest in the 1890s, response to the Great Depression in the 1930s—were long-lasting crises that had proved divisive enough to weaken the centrists within a party. Over time, polarizing forces had come into play in one or another party. Ultimately, realignments were played out in different ways depending on when the polarizing elements had gained control of a party and how the other party (or a third party) had responded. In the early 1970s, although the Vietnam war and issues of social permissiveness were boisterous and divisive, the only issue that held out the potential for party realignment, according to Sundquist, was race. Sundquist concluded that realignment was unlikely, foreseeing instead a continuing disintegration of the party system as partisan attachments continued to weaken. People jarred loose from past party loyalties would remain detached until a new set of issues rekindled political commitments.

Steiner's research focused on social policy. He produced a volume in 1971, *The State of Welfare,* which examined the politics of welfare reform, an especially timely subject given the decade of attention poverty programs had received under Democratic presidents and the recent push by Richard Nixon for the so-called family assistance plan. Steiner traced the evolution of aid to families with dependent children, veterans' non-service-connected pensions, food stamps, and public housing as well as the emerging militancy of welfare clients. Steiner regarded the Nixon administration's plans as an important step toward creating a better relief system but advocated putting a national floor under benefits and gradually bringing the poor up to the poverty line.

His later work in the 1970s focused on policy toward children. In *The Children's Cause* (1976), he looked at both public and private organizations concerned with the welfare of children, reminding both that proponents of children's programs had to address theoretical questions about public intervention into the traditionally private domain of the family. He found their language imprecise and hard to turn into policy. He was critical of leadership in and out of government for not settling upon even the most elemental priorities. As he looked at the institutions with responsibility for children's welfare, he found the cause of children in the hands of such fractured planning and administrative bodies that policy could not be developed wisely or practically.

One of the most contentious social issues of the 1970s was the use of busing to integrate the schools, and one of Brookings most controversial studies during the 1970s was Gary Orfield's *Must We Bus?* (1978). Orfield examined both the constitutional issues and the socioeconomic realities of residential segregation. After looking at the successes and difficulties of a number of school districts and the political and popular reaction to busing, especially in the wake of the Nixon administration's retreat from busing as a strategy, Orfield concluded that there was no alternative to busing if American society held to the goal of integration. He concluded that it was feasible, the costs slight, and no educational harm likely to result. Busing would require metropolitanwide programs as well as federal aid for busing plans. The policies, concluded Orfield, had to proceed in tandem with efforts to speed housing desegregation.

The politics of policymaking and the assessment of policy outcomes gave unity to the work of others in the Governmental Studies program. Martha Derthick's two principal studies in the 1970s examined intergovernmental relations and the politics of social security policymaking. Her volume *Between State and Nation: Regional Organizations of the United States* (1974) looked at such regional experiments in administration as the Tennessee Valley Authority and the Appalachian Regional Commission. She concluded that the accomplishments of regional institutions usually fell well short of their objectives, especially as instruments for federal executive coordination and decentralization. Her *Policymaking for Social Security* (1979) showed how the social security program had developed with relatively little resistance. Derthick argued, however, that more debate over the program's scope and purpose would be healthy. Donald L. Horowitz's *The Courts and Social Policy* (1977) documented the growing tendency of the courts to function as policymakers and criticized their capacities as such.

Complaints about government bureaucrats have been sounded since colonial days; they have been no less muted in the twentieth century. Patently obvious managerial deficiencies in federal agencies drove Progressive Era reformers to establish the Institute for Government Research and state and municipal counterparts concerned with administrative efficiency. By the 1970s complaints about federal bureaucracy and administrative competence had much to do with questions about the political control of the bureaucracy and the reach of government into the lives of citizens.

Herbert Kaufman's interest in bureaucracies took the form in the 1970s of two studies, one asking whether government organizations were immortal and the other examining red tape. In the former study Kaufman noted the impressive ability of government agencies to survive, but he found no ready solutions to either prevent their birth or hasten their death. His conclusions sounded a warning to public administrators that their tasks were going to be ever more complicated as the number of agencies grew.

Kaufman's 1977 study, *Red Tape: Its Origins, Uses and Abuses*, went to the heart of one of the most familiar complaints about large government organizations. Again he found no easy solutions to the problem of excessive paper work and procedures; one person's superfluous paper is simply another's procedural protection. Red tape is not, in and of itself, a measure of incompetence or bureaucracy gone amuck; it is the natural consequence of diversity, distrust, and democracy. Often it is a protection against the misuses of public money; it is a way of guaranteeing democratic influences on bureaucratic decisionmaking. Kaufman envisioned no sharp instrument to cut through all the red tape, but thought that with "the delicate wielding of a scalpel rather than furious flailing about with a meat ax" some of it might be trimmed away.

Hugh Heclo's study of politics and the civil service, *A Government of Strangers: Executive Politics in Washington* (1977), posed broad questions concerning political leadership within large governmental bureaucracies. How have the boundaries between political appointees and upper-level civil servants shifted over the years? Have career executives been politicized and political appointees bureaucratized? What are working relations like between the two groups? What are the limits of reform? He found no sharp political-bureaucratic delineation separating the 700 or so political appointees from the 7,000 top-level civil servants. Given their transience and lack of governmental experience, however, the political executives had little hope of winning control over their agencies. While political executives tend to be captured by their agencies, Heclo noted that career bureaucrats were becoming increasingly politicized. The venerable ideals of a civil service were thus endangered. Finding no management system that would allow political leaders to easily gain control of the bureaucracy, Heclo based his solutions on the reinvigoration of the civil service ideal, creating a group of executives more mobile than bureaucrats but less transient and politicized than political appointees.

Although studies of particular policies and bureaucratic questions generally followed the interests of individual scholars, the Governmental Studies program did put together a series of studies of the presidential selection process. As long ago as 1888 James Bryce had pondered the reasons why great men are not chosen presidents. Brookings scholars ranged over subjects that might hold out the answers, looking at campaign financing, the role of conventions, the electoral college, presidential campaigns, and third parties. Their studies analyzed political processes but did not come up with solutions to the age-old problem. Instead, the studies helped readers understand the complexity of democratic institutions and the nature of American political culture, arguing in general that procedural changes would be less consequential than reformers anticipated.

Donald Matthews, who had moved from Brookings and was teaching at the University of Washington, and his associate William R. Keech published *The Party's Choice* in 1976, the seventh volume in the Brookings series on presidential selection. Keech and Matthews undertook a detailed analysis of electoral reform, finding some merits in a nationally coordinated series of five or six primaries. On the whole, they concluded that rules make little difference. The determining factors in elections are social and economic structures, values and beliefs, communications and news, and political opportunity. In asking who presidential nominees were and why they had been selected, they found that changes in rules and procedures had relatively little to do with either expanding the pool of talent from which presidential candidates are drawn or determining the parties' eventual nominees. They argued that the proliferation of state primaries had tended merely to ratify the position of the front-runner rather than to serve as a genuinely open and competitive selection process, despite the McGovern nomination in 1972. Similarly, Stephen Hess argued in *The Presidential Campaign*, first published in 1974, that rules and procedural changes will not draw a different, potentially greater group of contenders into the presidential race.

Some of the most enduring books to emerge from the Governmental Studies program resulted from the scholarly assessment of democratic processes and bureaucratic structure. Yet the program took on other intellectual tasks. In the mid-1970s Steiner described three goals for the Governmental Studies program: "to provide a realistic explanation of public policymaking at the national government level; to evaluate structural aspects of the American governmental and political systems; and to examine substantive policy in practice—to monitor implementation, expose inflated claims of accomplishment (or confirm them), and the impediments to making results consistent with purposes."[10] There the agenda was set not by the enduring dilemmas of sound administration and democratic self-government but by a set of new government programs and immediate concerns about their execution.

The Laboratory of Government

In 1972, three years after Richard Nixon announced the New Federalism, Congress enacted a five-year general revenue sharing program that transferred about $5.3 billion per year to approximately 39,000 entities of state and local governments. The underlying assumption, which, in time, proved to be wrong, was that state and local revenues were likely to grow more slowly and federal revenues faster than their respective needs for expenditures.

The program, which survived until the Reagan administration abolished it, was the moderate Republicans' answer to the fragmentation and rigidity of the Great Society's categorical grant programs. (In fact, Walter Heller had unsuccessfully advocated a similar program during the Johnson administration.) During its fourteen-year life span, revenue sharing paid out more than $80 billion in essentially unrestricted grants. Along with a program of block grants, which combined funds from categorical aid programs, the flow of money to the states was designed to reverse the flow of power to Washington.

When the revenue sharing program was set up, officials from the Ford Foundation approached Brookings with an idea for evaluating the program (it was expected that government agencies would themselves provide funding as the project matured). The Monitoring Studies group, headed by Richard Nathan, was an effort to examine the effects of revenue sharing on states and localities. Nathan was intimately involved in the Nixon administration program from its inception, having first chaired the Nixon transition task force that recommended revenue sharing and then worked as assistant director of the Office of Management and Budget on the design and passage of the revenue sharing legislation.[11] Earlier in his career he had done a Brookings study, under contract to the U.S. Commission on Civil Rights, examining the Civil Rights Act of 1964 and focusing on organizational problems and statutory changes.

The group's first study, *Monitoring Revenue Sharing,* was published in 1975, in time for the House and Senate debates on whether to extend the program (a second volume followed in 1977). The research was based on case studies of sixty-five different jurisdictions, undertaken by twenty-seven field researchers. They looked at the effects of the money on local budgets and programs, tried to identify changes that might have been brought about in local political institutions, and examined Washington's mechanisms for distributing the money. The researchers wanted to know how the money was being used, discovering that more than half was used for new programs and the rest for tax relief or maintaining programs that would otherwise be cut. They also asked what its political effects were, learning that some jurisdictions had arranged for public revenue sharing hearings and more open budget processes. The Brookings research, far more systematic and rigorous than data collected by the Treasury Department or other federal agencies, gave substance to House and Senate debates on renewing the legislation in 1975 and 1976.

The New Federalism initiatives continued in the mid-1970s with block grants for community development and employment and job training; the Brookings team adapted its field evaluation methods to assess the new block grant programs.[12] For the Department of Housing and Urban Development the group looked at Community Development Block Grants (CDBG), a program set up in 1974 to consolidate seven other programs. The analysts, working in thirty central cities as well as twenty-five other locales receiving block grants, generally found the local officials competent in identifying needs and ensuring citizen participation. The group's second report to HUD, based on work in sixty-two communities, examined how such communities used their discretionary authority in expending federal funds. The group found that the communities tended to initiate fewer large-scale projects and to shift from social service delivery to neighborhood preservation. On the whole, the decisionmaking structures were broadened. The studies of the CDBG recommended changes in the formulas for allocating grants so that older, declining cities would receive more aid. Both the Ford and the Carter administrations found the changes meritorious, and they were written into the Housing and Community Development Act of 1977.

In 1976 the group began to look at the impact of the Emergency Jobs Program Act of 1976 for the National Commission for Manpower Policy. The basic question the group posed was whether federal funds increased overall public employment or were merely used to replace local funds. As the team of field associates was assembled, the Departments of Labor and Commerce asked for more research on job creation. Work under Richard Nathan (involving both Brookings and Princeton's Woodrow Wilson School) continued as field researchers monitored the use of funds in forty-two communities. They examined Titles II and VI of the Comprehensive Employment and Training Act, finding that four-fifths of the money created new jobs and that only one-fifth was used to forestall local tax increases.

The Monitoring Studies group, which relied on economists and political scientists in roughly equal numbers, devised and gradually refined methods for evaluating large-scale programs and their effects. The programs they studied did not present them with a neat and controlled laboratory environment (in fact, there were no controls at all against which to measure revenue sharing). The evaluation of full-scale programs already under way presented very different sets of intellectual problems for the analyst from those which confronted a policy planner designing a new program or a researcher examining a small-scale demonstration project. Brookings was well suited to serve as a monitor of government performance; it was capable of bringing together scholars from different disciplines who were able to scrutinize a program's economic and institutional effects, and it could mobilize a far-flung network of researchers.

The institution's concern for improving the standards of government performance—and the analytic methods of evaluation—was not limited to its monitoring studies team. The rush of legislation in the mid-1960s gave way to a more cautious, experimental approach to social policy by the decade's end. Social experiments in education, welfare policy, and health were set in motion. Each raised a number of questions about how to evaluate such experiments and how to refine government's experimental methods. Brookings began to look at social experiments in the mid-1970s when the Office of Economic Opportunity asked the institution to examine the use of incentive contracts in education. The analysis of that experiment, judged to be a flawed test, led to other evaluations of social experiments. Brookings scholars looked at compensatory education, housing allowances, and one of the most famous experiments of the period, the New Jersey Negative Income Tax experiment. Although the long-term prospects for using social experiments remained promising, contributors to the various Brookings volumes on social experimentation were well aware of the difficulty of using experimentally derived findings to guide policymakers and were also keenly concerned about the legal and ethical issues raised by such experiments.

The influence of analytic work, whether derived from systematic program evaluation, social experiments, or the solitary research of a single scholar, is always difficult to assess. The specific lines by which research findings are introduced into governmental deliberations by an outside research organization are always tenuous. Ideally, research should continually inform the policy process, but there are never any guarantees that it will be heeded by policymakers or that research findings will not be distorted or abused in policy debates.

Moreover, the lines through which research and analysis find their way into the policy process are diffuse. Institutions are connected to the process in diverse ways, and sometimes those linkages operate less like hard connective tissue than like nerve endings transmitting quick signals. In the early 1970s Brookings tried to look rigorously at its interaction with Congress.[13] Between 1971 and 1973 Brookings staff members had testified before Congress at twenty-four separate hearings, with several members sometimes appearing for the same hearings. The informal consultations were harder to tally, but one Brookings scholar had dealt with fifteen different senators, twelve representatives, and ten congressional staff members in the two-year period. Another counted fourteen senators, seven representatives, and twenty-four staff members among those with whom he had consulted informally. The estimate of the number of Brookings consultations with people on Capitol Hill produced an educated guess that there were between 500 and 1,000 contacts in a two-year period. Attendance at Brookings meetings was more precisely tallied, with four to eight senators and representatives showing up when seminars or study groups were organized for them. Seventy-five had attended various sessions of the Advanced Study program. Book requests from Capitol Hill were also tallied, with 308 members requesting copies of *Setting National Priorities* in 1973.

While the general patterns of interaction were clear (although precise measurement was next to impossible), no responsible social scientist would try to force conclusions about the direct causal relationships between research findings and policy outcomes. As Kermit Gordon observed, "The path along which it [policy research] affects decision-making is so tortuous that the trail usually becomes difficult or impossible to follow. Diligent investigation would assuredly uncover a few cases in which the causal nexus between study and decision is

direct and unambiguous; but these would clearly be in a small minority."
The network, which transmits (and sometimes distorts) research, is
composed of individuals working in policymaking posts as well as an
array of private research institutions, governmental advisory staffs,
popular journalistic media, and interest groups. "In the end," Gordon
observed, "the initiative may be decisive in inspiring an important
policy decision, but it will have been strained through so many filters
and combined with so many other ingredients that the causal chain
may be untraceable."[14]

When Brookings monitors governmental performance, the causal
chain may indeed be forged of so many small and tangled links that
the direct impact of analytic insights upon political decisionmaking
becomes untraceable. But that is not the only arena in which Brookings
operates. The institution's scholars have also invented new analytic tools,
offered theoretical insights, and addressed the underlying intellectual
assumptions of public policy. That larger causal chain, affecting elite
opinion and longer-term scholarly developments, stretches away from
governmental offices and the arena of practical politics. While Brookings
has been a monitor of policies and programs and its scholars are
inevitably engaged in the day-to-day discussion of contemporary
issues, the institution must nourish itself intellectually by maintaining
connections with the scholarly community. It must ask questions about
broader policy assumptions and the intellectual tools at hand for
thinking about policy questions. Indeed, one of the constant concerns
among Brookings scholars has been to maintain the balance in their
research program between the immediacy of practical policy concerns
and the quest for better analytic tools and theoretical insights.

5

PUBLIC POLICY TOOLS

INTELLECTUAL MIGRATIONS in the wake of a presidential election are not uncommon in Washington. The proliferation of think tanks over the past two decades certainly has facilitated such moves, although the number of people involved has never been especially large. For Brookings in the late 1960s, the arrival of economists who had held key policy advisory positions, Arthur M. Okun, Henry J. Aaron, and Charles L. Schultze, greatly augmented the Economic Studies program.

Just as Steiner brought the Governmental Studies program to a new level, Kermit Gordon and Joseph A. Pechman assembled a group of economists who would set new intellectual standards for the institution, yielding broadly conceived works on macroeconomic theory, a new professional journal, an important body of work on government regulation of the economy, and a well-received annual series scrutinizing the federal budget and the president's policy priorities.

Okun was arguably the leading theorist of the group. He had been a student of Arthur Burns at Columbia, where he received his undergraduate and graduate degrees. He joined the Yale University faculty in 1952 and rose to full professor over the ensuing decade. James Tobin, his friend and colleague in New Haven, arranged for him to consult with the Council of Economic Advisers in 1961 and later to move to Washington as a staff economist working on forecasting and fiscal policy. In 1964 he replaced Walter Heller on the council, succeeding Gardner Ackley as chairman in 1968. Kermit Gordon lured him to Brookings as the Johnson administration came to an end, urging Okun to stay in Washington for a six-month trial marriage with the institution. Gordon wanted him to write about his policymaking experiences "while the memories were fresh and the wounds unhealed."[1] He remained at Brookings, producing three books in the twelve years before his death in 1980 at the age of fifty-one.

His first Brookings work was *The Political Economy of Prosperity* (1970), which reviewed the course of policymaking in the 1960s. Okun analyzed the fiscal policy successes early in the decade and explained how the defense buildup and the failure to enact a tax increase in 1966 had caused fiscal policy to veer off course. The "new economics" was defeated by the "old politics," he argued, and the continuing failure to raise taxes had made it increasingly difficult for both fiscal and monetary tools to dampen demand. With neither fiscal nor monetary tools entirely adequate, he called for labor and business voluntarily to restrain wage demands and price increases. He also recommended that a nonpartisan advisory board act as a kind of economic umpire to "call foul balls" when wages and prices were out of bounds. Anticipating the increasingly politicized policymaking environment of the 1970s, he also urged economists to set out clearly their areas of nonpartisan and bipartisan agreement, wondering whether a new advisory group might need to be set up to report to Congress.

His *Equality and Efficiency: The Big Tradeoff* (1975) was a self-described attempt to find out what he really believed in an increasingly conservative political environment. "Maybe I began to worry about myself; it almost looked as if the slightly left-of-center liberal that I am is a vanishing breed. Yet I hadn't turned conservative and I hadn't turned radical, and I felt that those of us who think of ourselves as the heirs of the New Deal liberal creed have a message and still can defend the faith."[2] The book, based on his Godkin lectures at Harvard in 1974, looked at the perpetual tension between the egalitarian principles that are at the center of political democracy and the underlying inequality that drives the capitalist system. Making the case for capitalism (offering "two cheers" three years before Irving Kristol), Okun explored the values fostered by markets—decentralized decisionmaking, efficiency, experimentation, and innovation. He warned, however, that the pursuit of efficiency sanctioned inequality, even to the point of undermining individual rights. Having looked throughout his career at the trade-off between inflation and employment, he asked about the larger social and political trade-offs between efficiency and equality.

The short volume had no pretensions about providing a detailed outline of remedies, but it did offer a principle to guide the inevitable compromises between the two legitimate ends of equality and efficiency, namely, that any sacrifice of one ought to bring about a much greater enhancement of the other. Between Milton Friedman's emphasis on efficiency and John Rawls's focus on equality, Okun insisted on the inescapable tension between the two values and challenged society to continue to search for ways of drawing and redrawing the boundary between "the domain of rights and the domain of the dollar."[3]

His final Brookings work was a posthumous volume, *Prices and Quantities: A Macroeconomic Analysis* (1981). When reviewing Okun's book, MIT's Robert Solow recalled a story about his own father, a furrier, who had once remarked sadly on examining a collection of exquisite sable skins that it was a pity that only a connoisseur could know how good they really were. "A layman cannot possibly know what a good economist Arthur Okun was," he added. He was always an elegant writer and phrasemaker, coining terms—"discomfort index," "leaky bucket," and "invisible handshake"—that brought economic abstractions vividly to mind both in his writing and in his frequent congressional testimony.

In his final scholarly work he returned to aggregative economics— the effort to understand the forces that govern the general level of prices, the amount of real output, and unemployment. He was trying to understand why the confident assumptions of fiscal theorists in the 1960s no longer seemed to hold, having failed to account for the phenomenon of "stagflation" in the 1970s. Traditional models of macroeconomic change had always assumed short-run flexibility in prices and wages, but such flexibility no longer seemed operable. Macroeconomic policy tools, which had worked when policymakers needed expansionary measures, seemed unable to restrain the economy in periods of inflation.

Okun asked why the textbook assumptions about short-run wage and price flexibility were erroneous. He tested Keynesian, monetarist, and "rational expectations" models against the workings of both modern labor and product markets, asking what caused such markets not to respond quickly to changing economic conditions. Looking at market relationships, whether between buyer and seller or worker and employer, Okun found that prices were related more to cost than to fluctuations in demand and that neither wages nor the work force tended to be cut quickly in periods of slack demand. The desire to preserve relationships with customers and to protect long-time employees prevented wages and prices from fluctuating as they might in a more fluid "auction" market. Okun concluded that the implicit agreements in both product and labor markets to leave prices and wages intact constituted an "invisible handshake" and made prices insensitive to short-term eco- nomic fluctuations. For policymakers looking for a way out of the swamp of stagflation, Okun assembled a menu of measures, recommend- ing fiscal and monetary restraints along with a tax-based incomes policy.

Okun's theoretical work in the 1970s was complemented by other

Brookings projects geared toward understanding the worldwide phenomenon of inflation as well as domestic measures for controlling prices and wages. In August 1971 President Nixon imposed a ninety-day freeze on wages, prices, and rents that set in motion a series of anti-inflation programs. Brookings encouraged several economists, especially some who had been directly involved in policy implementation, to analyze the successes and failures of the administration's measures. A series of volumes looked at the history of presidential exhortation and controls as well as at more immediate policy assumptions; other books scrutinized the jerry-built administrative apparatus erected in the early 1970s.[4]

With macroeconomic theory and policymaking under siege, Brookings embarked on a project that would bring together members of the institution's staff with academic economists in a regular forum to consider what Gordon called the "puzzles" of economic performance. Economists such as Gordon and Okun, who had been a part of the policymaking process, felt that the institution needed a vehicle for addressing immediate issues in a more timely fashion than the book-length study. Indeed, there is a continuing tension in the minds of many Brookings scholars between the book as the primary institutional product and the shorter report or journal article.

In 1970, with support from the Sloan and Walker foundations, Okun and George L. Perry, an economist trained at the Massachusetts Institute of Technology who left the University of Minnesota to come to Brookings, organized the Brookings Panel on Economic Activity. A group of thirteen economists (four on the Brookings staff) planned to meet three times each year to discuss papers that might shed light on some of the most pressing issues of the moment and to hear analysis by specialists knowledgeable about particular sectors of the economy. The *Brookings Papers on Economic Activity* contained the papers and salient aspects of the discussion. The first volume, published in April 1970, examined such topics as the reasons for the burst of inflation in

1969, the puzzling phenomenon of increased housing starts in the face of tight money, and the concept of the "full-employment surplus."

From the outset the *Brookings Papers on Economic Activity* was intended to be more accessible than equation-laden academic journals. The journal has relied on the editors' interpretive essays that introduce each volume and the inclusion of queries and clarifying observations of fellow panel members to put the articles in context and to explain analytic problems to nonspecialists. Within a few years the *Brookings Papers on Economic Activity* was one of the most widely read journals among business economists and economic policy analysts. While the volumes focus on current problems affecting economic growth and price stability, they also address theoretical questions and offer new empirical findings that are relevant to the policymaker or business executive. The *Brookings Papers* are the most academic of the institution's regular publications and are viewed by the institution's economists as a vital link to the academic world, especially to younger university-based economists.

In revisiting old policy terrain, Brookings found a far larger audience for another new venture that began early in the 1970s. During the fifty-odd years since the passage of the Budget and Accounting Act of 1921, the budget process had become the focal point for determining national goals and choosing among policy strategies. In selecting among programs and policy means, analytic techniques had undergone consid-erable refinement since the days of Harding, Coolidge, and the first generation of researchers at the Institute for Government Research. By the 1960s social science tools for appraising new programs had won wide acceptance, best symbolized by President Johnson's 1965 Executive Order requiring domestic agencies of the federal government to use the planning, programming, and budgeting system introduced into Robert McNamara's Defense Department in the early 1960s. Brookings staff members had not only served in the Bureau of the Budget (now the Office of Management and Budget), they were students of both the budget process and the policy analytic techniques employed there.

Charles Schultze was assistant director of the bureau from 1962 to 1965 under Kermit Gordon and then director before moving to Brookings in 1968. He witnessed firsthand the reception by government agencies of the new policy analytic techniques, especially the planning, programming, and budgeting system (PPBS) that sought to bring analytic and quantitative discipline to the selection and implementation of policy options.

His initial work at Brookings began with an exploration of the intersection between social science and politics. In *The Politics and Economics of Public Spending* (originally delivered as the 1968 Gaither Lectures in Systems Science at the University of California, Berkeley), Schultze looked at how the efficiency and effectiveness criteria of the PPBS worked in the real world of political decisionmaking, where adversarial bargaining was the accepted method for resolving disagreements. He argued that economists' analytical methods, though often criticized as unrealistic and abstract, could serve to discipline the bargaining and compromise that are central to the political process. He also discussed the design and implementation of public programs, asking policymakers to think carefully about relating the incentives built into programs to the institutional interests at stake. Seeing the complexity and interrelatedness of problems, he also explored the need for new administrative structures to foster cooperation among officials from various jurisdictions and functional agencies.

Schultze and his colleagues had come to appreciate—in ways that perhaps they had not fully understood in the early 1960s—that the use of sophisticated planning techniques and the analysis of programs, no matter how scientific and technically rigorous, are imbedded in a political environment. They realized that the entire budgetmaking process is a set of political decisions. In fact, the president's budget is an argument for certain goals and priorities, though not in a form or language that is easily accessible or that sets out clear alternatives and their long-term consequences. As Schultze explained, "Precisely because it must advocate the course recommended by the President, the budget cannot emphasize the difficulty of the choices made. It records the President's decisions, but it does not identify the close ones. Alternatives that were serious contenders for adoption but were finally rejected are seldom if ever mentioned. . . . [T]he budget is a document designed to persuade an independent Congress rather than to analyze policy alternatives."[5]

While budget debates in the 1960s had often focused on the total expenditures—especially as the budget passed the $100 billion barrier—it is in the fiscal detail that the broader political course of the nation is charted. One of the tasks that Schultze and his colleagues set for themselves in the 1970s was to translate the implicit budget decisions into a form that would be accessible and debatable. They started one of the institution's most successful and widely read series of the 1970s, a series that after a hiatus in the 1980s would be revived and refocused to address the budget debates of the 1990s. In the 1970s the *Setting National Priorities* series looked each year at the federal budget's overall economic impact and examined the alternatives to and the consequences of the choices implicit in the president's budget.

Appearing about four months after the president submitted his budget to Congress, the volumes put the president's policy priorities in context, offering five-year projections based on different economic and expenditure assumptions. The series, funded initially by the Carnegie Corporation, ran from 1971 to 1984. In the early 1970s, with executive and legislative branches locked in controversy over budget impoundments and with the process of budgetmaking in disarray, the Brookings studies found a wide audience. The annual volumes proved invaluable to members of Congress and others following the budget debate during the heated contest between executive and legislative branches in the early 1970s. The series was an instrument of education in the widest sense, informing Congress, journalists, and the interested public about the budget process. At its peak over 30,000 copies of each volume were sold.

While its impact on the debate each year was simply to make the implicit policy choices more apparent and to register the arguments for and against various programs, after only a few years its cumulative effect was to propel Congress to set up its own analytic agency, the Congressional Budget Office, created by the Congressional Budget and Impoundment Control Act of 1974. Once the Congressional Budget Office and its staff got to work—Brookings senior fellow Alice Rivlin was selected as its first director—the annual volumes in the Brookings series were largely superseded as budget analyses. While proving to be less important to the Washington community and the annual budget debate, they nonetheless continued to enjoy strong classroom sales.

While Schultze encountered the new tools of policy analysis during his term at the Budget Bureau, his colleague Alice Rivlin, a graduate of Bryn Mawr and recipient of a Ph.D. in economics from Radcliffe, had worked as assistant secretary for planning and evaluation at the Department of Health, Education, and Welfare in the 1960s. There she had seen a small analytic office of five people grow into a fifty-person department. They had been pioneers in bringing cost-effectiveness techniques into the realm of social policy. Her 1971 book, *Systematic Thinking for Social Action* (based on the 1970 Gaither lectures at Berkeley), was a close look at what cost-benefit analysis had taught about efforts to address poverty, education, and health. Taking stock of what had been learned through the use of better survey techniques and the then novel applications of computers, she concluded that a great deal had been learned about the dimensions of social problems, as well as about the precise costs and distribution of benefits of social programs. Analysts had better insights into the deficiencies of current programs and much improved tools for comparing the costs of various proposals for change. The new techniques had not proved useful, however, in comparing the benefits of different kinds of social programs—investments in health programs versus investments in education, for example—nor had they yet revealed much about how to improve the workings of social service programs.

Although the hopes of reformers and social scientists had been high for some fifty years, policy analysts could not yet offer certain knowledge about social causes and effects, if indeed they ever would. Rivlin offered a tempered, realistic view of what analysis could accomplish, calling for more systematic and longer-term study of programs already in place, with a view toward improving measures of performance. Moreover, she recommended major new experimental efforts in social policymaking rather than the random innovation that was so characteristic of American social reform.

The 1970s saw a waning of faith in the uses of the social sciences in public policymaking. The expectations in the 1960s were excessive, but as Charles Schultze suggests, "It was a mixture of too much faith as well as misplaced faith; there were mistaken beliefs about what social science can do." While the work of Okun, Schultze, and Rivlin offered a chastened appraisal of the uses of knowledge in the political process as they looked at cost-benefit analyses and large-scale social experiments and explored the limits of theoretical knowledge in the social sciences, they did not retreat altogether from the conviction that such insights could ultimately serve the political process. But would such insights be used? Far more worrisome was the apparent repudiation of experts and their expertise by political leaders and the public.

Henry Aaron tackled the subject of the experts and their political role in his *Politics and the Professors: The Great Society in Perspective* (1978). A senior fellow at Brookings since 1968, Aaron was serving in the Carter administration as HEW's assistant secretary for planning and evaluation when the book appeared, although he returned to Brookings within the year. Seeing the public's much diminished faith in government's ability to plan and administer programs, he examined the part played by social science experts in the legislative outpouring of the 1960s. He looked at what scholars had contributed to the understanding of poverty and discrimination, education, and unemployment and inflation.

He found a curious reversal of the presumed causal relationship between scholarly ideas and public policy. Scholarly insights often followed changes in policy rather than preceded them. Moreover, scholarly work typically made little direct contribution to the development of policy. In the 1960s social science research—often in its crudest formulation—had influence primarily because it reinforced popular attitudes about what government ought to be doing. The widespread conviction that government could act wisely and well in the 1960s had corresponded with growing confidence in what social scientists knew about society and the economy, but the programs of the Great Society were not the result of professorial proselytizing or lobbying.

Although social scientists found themselves blamed for the perceived failure of Great Society programs, the loss of faith in government in the 1970s, Aaron argued, had arisen from the disillusionment over Vietnam and Watergate and the dissolution of the civil rights movement as it moved from a legal agenda to an economic and social one. Moreover, the intellectual consensus on how to cope with poverty, unemployment, and inflation collapsed as social scientists turned their critical gaze (and analytic tools) toward examination of the efficacy of the myriad new programs of the 1960s. What Aaron found was a community of social scientists rife with internal disagreement and professionally inclined to challenge research results and methods. Social scientists were seldom capable of agreeing long enough for a political consensus to take shape. Thus, social science knowledge, far from spurring the nation toward action, now served to corrode any consensus upon which governmental policies might be built.

Aaron's insights exposed the underlying tension between organized social science inquiry and political action, and he raised fundamental questions about the uses of research in decisionmaking processes. In the final analysis, he wondered whether research was inherently corrosive of the political enthusiasms that give rise to social and economic reform.

Implicit in Aaron's work are some of the recurring questions upon which a serious policy research institution like Brookings must constantly reflect. When is knowledge about social and economic matters certain enough to guide policy decisions? How do analytic findings best serve a decisionmaking process that ultimately depends upon political and moral judgments? Who is the audience for the kinds of research that Brookings undertakes? How is research best communicated? How can the uncertainties inherent in honest social science inquiry be conveyed in a political arena where arguments must be set out with trenchant conviction and minimal overt doubt? The interplay of social science research and the policymaking process offers no simple models or formulas. It is easy to say that Brookings is a bridge between disparate worlds, but the means of constructing the bridge and organizing the traffic on it are problems that require constant engineering and occasional redesign.

One of Brookings most successful programs in the era of waning faith in government and social science research was its body of research on government's regulation of economic activity. In exploring economic regulation Brookings was looking not at new and hastily conceived social programs but at one of the long-standing functions of the federal government. That role was embodied early on in the Interstate Commerce Act of 1887 and continued in the work of regulatory agencies that had been functioning for many decades.

The Brookings research project began in 1967 as a three-year effort to evaluate governmental practices in regulating such industries as energy, communication, and transportation. Ford Foundation support, which totaled $1.8 million between 1967 and 1975, turned the undertaking into a project comparable in scale to the earlier work on government finance. In its first phase it yielded twenty-two books and monographs, sixty-five journal articles, and thirty-eight dissertations. Over the years the intellectual work that began at Brookings and on university campuses—and was taken up by other Washington-based research institutions in the 1970s—helped demonstrate the costliness and inefficiency of much of the government's regulatory activity. It shaped a growing consensus among professional economists that by the mid-1970s had come to embrace consumer activists, business executives, and bipartisan political leadership. The research on government regulation is one of the institution's premier collaborative efforts and an exemplary case of how academic ideas ultimately make their way in the policy process. While other research institutions engaged in the movement for deregulation in the 1970s, Brookings was more concerned with channeling the research interests of scores of economists in a new direction than with disseminating ideas to policymakers and popular constituencies.

Brookings initial program of regulatory studies drew a sizable corps of younger economists into the study of particular regulated industries. In doing so, and as Ford Foundation staff members had expected it would, the research project helped redress some of the long-standing imbalances in the discipline of economics. The intellectual allure of Keynes's *General Theory* in the late 1930s had drawn bright young scholars toward macroeconomic studies. With the practical realities of national economic policymaking focused on fiscal policy, for nearly thirty years many of the most talented members of the profession had concentrated on macroeconomic questions. Indeed, macroeconomic concerns since the 1930s had virtually eliminated the venerable American tradition of institutional economics and had left microeconomic work underdeveloped within the profession. The Brookings program of regulatory studies helped create a new pool of professional manpower concerned with microeconomic matters. Moreover, by drawing scholars and graduate students into the field, giving them outlets for publication and discussion, and forging links between scholars and policymakers, the regulatory studies opened the way for experts to advise legislators and work within the regulatory agencies as the movement toward deregulation gained momentum in the 1970s.

The work at Brookings ranged across several industries, including transportation, communications, public power, and energy. The first volume on regulation was Ann F. Friedlaender's *The Dilemma of Freight Transport Regulation* (1969). Underscoring the deficiencies of the Interstate Commerce Act of 1887, which had been passed when rail transport was the primary means of carrying freight, Friedlaender calculated that the Interstate Commerce Commission's outmoded regulations cost the U.S. economy approximately $500 million in direct costs for shipping and production and an incalculable sum in indirect costs. Other studies of transportation regulation included George Eads's work on local service airlines and George W. Douglas and James C. Miller III's study of domestic air transport. Roger Noll, Merton Peck, and John McGowan examined television regulation. Noll also edited a later volume that explored the relationship between government regulation and professional sports. Individual regulatory agencies were studied in such works as Stephen Breyer and Paul MacAvoy's critique of the Federal Power Commission (FPC) and the consequences of that agency's regulation of natural gas, gas pipelines, and electric power. Their study found few benefits to the consumer resulting from the FPC's regulatory efforts and added to the growing body of evidence that regulatory commissions were clumsy instruments for pursuing economic goals. More theoretical concerns were addressed in edited volumes on technological innovations and their diffusion in regulated industries and on the means of promoting competition.

By the mid-1970s the initial program on the regulation of economic activity had ended but not before creating a body of work that, because of its analytic weight, began to tug against the framework of federal economic regulation. Economic analysis demonstrated the net costs of regulation in potentially competitive markets, pressing the case for increased competition and an end to price and entry regulation. Charles Schultze's *The Public Use of Private Interest,* a book based on his 1976 Godkin lectures at Harvard University and one of Brookings all-time best-selling volumes, summarized the economists' case against the century-old regulatory structures. Government had come to rely on a cumbersome assemblage of laws that often achieved the opposite of their intended effects. Taxes and other devices, Schultze argued, ought to be used to create marketlike incentives to encourage desirable behavior.

Analysis is rarely persuasive in and of itself, and it cannot determine the precise course and timing of policy decisions. In this instance, however, the regulatory studies struck resonant political chords. The consumer movement, growing concern about inflation and business competitiveness, and bipartisan presidential and senatorial leadership gave political impetus to the intellectual work. While Brookings and its university collaborators shaped the initial intellectual movement, other institutions picked up the banner, waved it more vigorously, and garnered much of the credit for promoting deregulation in the 1970s. Nonetheless, Brookings continued to address regulatory questions after the initial Ford grant ended. Brookings scholars turned to studies of social and environmental regulation and, by the 1980s, were assessing the consequences of deregulation.

Though no other series was as large as the studies of regulation and government finance, a cluster of work organized under the theme of "social economics" brought the analytic tools of the economist to bear on social programs. It included Alan Sorkin's book on American Indians and federal aid, Robert D. Reischauer and Robert W. Hartman's study of school finance, and Henry Aaron's books on federal housing policy and the obstacles to welfare reform. Brookings economists also looked at public employee unions in a series that included *The Unions and the Cities* by Harry H. Wellington and Ralph K. Winter, Jr., and *Public Employee Unionism: Structure, Growth, Policy* by Jack Stieber.

One of the institution's most innovative departures in the early 1970s was a study of the Japanese economy. *Asia's New Giant: How the Japanese Economy Works* (1976) was a direct result of Kermit Gordon's interest in studying the economies of other countries, which Brookings had begun with its 1968 volume *Britain's Economic Prospects*. Henry Rosovsky and Hugh Patrick oversaw this collaboration between area specialists and economists as they produced the first important English-language study of the Japanese economic miracle and how it came about. The team they directed in conjunction with the Japan Economic Research Center drew in non-Japanists such as Edward Denison, Richard Caves, and Lawrence Krause. With Japanese collaborators, they produced volumes on Japanese industrial organization and the sources of Japanese economic growth. Like the work in regulation, the Japanese studies helped direct intellectual talent into a field relatively neglected to that point by American academics.

Over the long term, one of the institution's principal influences has been to deepen the reservoirs of policy expertise, drawing young scholars into applied research projects when such topics are neglected by the universities, offering an institutional base for scholars who might otherwise orient their work toward discipline-driven theoretical problems, and linking researchers across several fields when their collective expertise might illuminate an emerging issue. It is not a function that leads necessarily to an immediate impact on executive decisions or legislative acts, but it is arguably the most important function that an applied research institution can play. It is the precondition for informed and carefully implemented policy change as well as for the constant monitoring, evaluation, and adjustment of policies and programs.

In fostering such networks Brookings is engaged in a delicate balancing act. Research at Brookings must be measured by the policy community's standards of practicality, timeliness, and relevance, while at the same time the research must strive to pass the academic community's tests of theoretical significance, technical proficiency, and empirical soundness. As an institution, Brookings is dependent on the university community for continuing theoretical advances and for intellectual personnel. At the same time it serves as a practically oriented, problem-driven research center where professional rewards and career patterns differ markedly from those of most university scholars. Brookings occupies a mediating position, partaking of both the scholarly and the political worlds. Not surprisingly, its role in the middle leads to considerable misunderstanding. In the fractious political environment existing since the late 1960s, the image and ideological identity of Brookings have frequently been misinterpreted by outside observers.

6

IMAGE AND IDEOLOGY

ALTHOUGH THINK TANKS now abound in the United States, even the most prominent are typically known to the public by little more than journalistic tag lines. A parenthetic phrase will describe a research center in a newspaper article; a brief sentence will reveal the institutional affiliation of the author of an op-ed essay. Such terse labels tend to stamp institutions with almost indelible ideological or partisan identities.

On occasion a phrase in an article or book review might suggest something more about the think tank's presumed role and influence. Brookings has been described variously as a "schoolmaster to government," "a powerhouse of economic thought," the "dean of public policy institutes," a place inhabited by "cool-eyed scholars" and "sober, grey-flanneled nonpartisans." It has been seen as a "blue-ribbon establishment institution," the "foundation of foundations," a "fortress of dispassion," and a "bastion of non-ideology." It has been portrayed as a place "operated by and for the elite," where intellectuals enjoy "hovering rights near the seat of government," or, more blithely, where "eggheads see the sunny-side." The tone of Brookings studies is routinely described as sober, careful, rigorous, measured, reliable, and dispassionate, although sometimes commentators suggest that one or another book shades toward the overly cautious or bland. But the phrase that has been most routinely used to characterize Brookings since the late 1960s is "the liberal, Democratic research institution," or some variation of those words.[1]

Perceptions

The label and the image are rooted in certain political realities of the 1960s and 1970s. Kermit Gordon and many of his colleagues had served in Democratic administrations during the 1960s. With Republicans in the White House in 1969 and after, the institution was widely perceived as a Democratic government in exile. The partisan reputation was not diminished in the mid-1970s when at least eight members of the Brookings staff joined the Carter administration.

Moreover, as national politics turned more sharply to the right in the 1970s, a number of conservative research and advocacy institutions clamored to the forefront of the public policy debate. They billed themselves as conservative counterparts to Brookings, modeling some of their activities on those of Brookings and aspiring to advisory relationships like those that Brookings had enjoyed during the 1960s. They also sought to strengthen the networks of conservative policy expertise.

In part, the Brookings Institution's liberal reputation was a matter of being outflanked by a cluster of organizations on the right. In part, the reputation was a matter of being closely identified with the technocratic liberal style of the 1960s. And in part, it was a matter of housing scholars who were outspoken critics of specific policies, especially the war in Vietnam.

Kermit Gordon and several members of the board were troubled by early signs of a deteriorating relationship between Brookings and the Nixon White House. While Brookings maintained its traditionally cordial working relations with various executive agencies and departments, Gordon sensed the hostility emanating from certain members of the president's staff. Presidential assistant H. R. Haldeman had written a memo as early as May 1969 saying that "the President wants to issue an order to all White House staff people (I will have to do this verbally) as well as to Cabinet people (also have to be done verbally) that they are not to use Brookings Institution."[2]

Some White House staff members were obsessed by the relationship between Brookings and Congress and the presence on the Brookings staff of several vocal critics of the administration's foreign policy. The White House eyed the institution's research suspiciously and regarded its briefing sessions and seminars as politically motivated and relentlessly hostile affairs. Early on, proposals were laid out by relatively low-level White House staff members to use the Internal Revenue Service to intimidate some of the more critical think tanks and foundations. Those plans stalled, however, when senior White House advisers concluded that top-level IRS staff members were not politically reliable enough to carry out the assignment discreetly. Nonetheless, Patrick Buchanan, then a Nixon speech writer, went to work on a series of tough speeches for Vice President Spiro Agnew attacking Brookings, the Ford Foundation, and other tax-exempt organizations that were considered to be the pillars of the liberal establishment.

In 1971 some White House staff members were certain that Leslie Gelb, a Brookings fellow and a friend of Daniel Ellsberg, had secreted away parts of the so-called Pentagon Papers and other Defense Department reports in his Brookings office. Nixon was furious. "I saw absolutely no reason for that report [on Johnson's 1968 bombing halt] to be at Brookings, and I said I wanted it back right now—even if it meant having to get it surreptitiously."[3] His aides proposed to "play the game tough," perhaps stealing the documents and covering their break-in by fire-bombing the institution, a plan attributed to Charles Colson, who denied involvement, and apparently halted by John Ehrlichman and John Dean. "There are a number of ways we could handle this," wrote another staff member. "There are risks in all of them, of course; but there are also risks in allowing this government in exile to grow increasingly arrogant and powerful as each day goes by."[4]

Despite the tough talk from the White House, conservatives there and on Capitol Hill saw Brookings primarily as a model to be emulated. Some members of the White House staff thought they could use Georgetown's Center for Strategic and International Studies or the American Enterprise Institute "to play the Brookings game." "One able guy on the outside with a little money and some real help from here could handle this task with ease," suggested one aide to Haldeman.[5] As another member of the president's staff put it, "If we are to build an enduring Republican Majority, then we need to construct institutes that will serve as the repository of its political beliefs. The Left has the Brookings Institution, tax-exempt, well-financed and funded—sort of a permanent political government-in-exile for liberal bureaucrats and Democratic professionals."[6]

Gordon worked as best he could to counter the image of Brookings as a partisan and ideological institution relentlessly critical of Nixon programs. He perceived two factions within the Nixon administration and very different reactions to Brookings from each of them. The substantive, technically oriented people in executive agencies proved quite willing to work with Brookings researchers on particular projects. Richard Nathan, while still on the Brookings staff, had chaired Nixon's transition task force on revenue sharing. Nixon's welfare reform proposal, the family assistance plan, had also relied on analysis from

Brookings staff members. However, the most conservative, politically oriented members of the White House staff had another view, seeing Brookings primarily as a partisan political enterprise.

In 1971 Gordon appealed to Peter Flanigan, a presidential assistant, asking for a mere ten-minute meeting with the president. Gordon was sure he could clear up the misconceptions about Brookings. Brookings scholars, he contended, supported the administration's policies about as often as they opposed them. Moreover, he pointed out that several administration officials had recently read and praised Brookings studies. It was consequently "a bit ungracious of people in the White House and the Executive Office to disparage Brookings as a partisan institution which is hostile to the Administration. Not only ungracious—untrue."[7]

Nonetheless, there were questions of image that had to be confronted as well as very hard questions about the limits of political involvement of Brookings staff members. Gordon had expressed fears, both privately and publicly, that some of his colleagues had been too politically active during the 1968 campaign.[8] He reiterated that they were involved as individuals, not as members of the institution, but he also knew that complicated issues involving academic freedom and First Amendment rights were at stake.

Gordon raised the general question of whether, in practice, there ought to be some limitations on the political utterances or partisan activities of Brookings staff members. Under existing rules, staff members had to make it clear that they spoke and wrote as individuals and were not taking an institutional position. Brookings publications then carried, as they do now, a standard disclaimer to that effect. If there were ever doubts about whether a staff member's political involvement violated the letter or spirit of provisions of the Tax Reform Act of 1969 governing the political activities of nonprofit organizations, the work had to be done on the staff member's own time.

In fact, the various writing, speaking, and advisory roles of Brookings staff members are always hard to compartmentalize and to monitor.

The institution's most fundamental objective is to see that its research reaches political leaders, provides intellectual guidance, enters political discourse, and has an impact on decisionmaking. Whether or not the Brookings researcher speaks as an individual or volunteers a formulaic disclaimer, an affiliation with Brookings adds authority to what is said and the institution is inevitably implicated, for better and for worse, in the individual's speaking, writing, and advising.

The trustees were no less concerned than Gordon about the institution's political and ideological image. For some of them, the solution lay in assembling a staff with a broader range of views. Some trustees also argued that a position on the Brookings staff was perhaps a unique responsibility—and the institution's public standing so in need of protection from charges of partisanship—that scholars should forgo any overt partisan commitments. Throughout the early 1970s, at meeting after meeting with the trustees, Gordon expressed his continuing concerns about the institution's image. He thought he might deflect some of the administration's hostility by agreeing to accept an appointment as a member of the Pay Board. He also persisted in arguing that Brookings was not especially hostile to the Nixon administration, and in 1971 he supplied George Shultz with a memo outlining forty-one instances in which Brookings staff members had supported administration policies.

But the continuing problem led to the creation of a special Brookings committee, chaired by Charles Schultze, to establish guidelines for outside political activities. The committee, which presented its report in January 1972, had no difficulty in concluding that there should be restrictions on campaigning and lobbying. Not only did the Tax Reform Act of 1969 set limits, but it was also clear that such activities harmed the institution's reputation for fairness and objectivity. Electoral involvement aside, such activities as briefing senators and representatives or speaking to various organizations were a part of the public service obligation of scholars engaged in policy research.

Nevertheless, some fine distinctions had to be drawn. The committee realized that unlike a university, where a professor's publishing and speaking are seldom construed as representing a university stance on an issue, a policy research institution was closer to the day-to-day political process and more liable to be identified with its staff members' policy proposals (especially when the institution's press published the book). The Brookings name and affiliation gave weight and credibility to its staff members' pronouncements. Nonetheless, the image of the institution as a place of nonpartisan and objective work had to be a matter of long-term concern to all who worked there. The committee endorsed the view that a better balance on the staff would serve to protect the institution from charges of bias, contending that in time a widely recognized diversity of views would ultimately give all scholars working there wider latitude to participate in political activities.

"Doctrinal balance" was the phrase Gordon and the board used as new staff members were recruited in the early 1970s. Gordon argued smartly that "it sharpens a man's thinking to have a colleague in the next office who disagrees with him."[9] Among those who joined Brookings after service in the Nixon administration were Philip Trezise, a career State Department official who had been assistant secretary of state for economic affairs from 1969 to 1971; C. Fred Bergsten, a senior staff member of the National Security Council; Stephen Hess, chairman of the White House Conference on Children and Youth; James Reichley, who had been on the White House staff; and Richard Nathan, who returned to Brookings after holding several positions in the Nixon administration.

The staff acquired a more bipartisan cast but it was still composed primarily of moderates regardless of party affiliation. Henry Aaron observed that the range of views at Brookings (whether Republican or Democratic) spans the center of the political spectrum—from roughly K to P in the political alphabet, as he puts it. In the final analysis, the staff tends to be made up of people drawn to public service or policy research by something other than strongly partisan or ideological commitments.

In 1973 the institution compiled a report on the public service of its staff under Kennedy, Johnson, and Nixon. The figures do not distinguish among different levels of government service or length of appointments. Nonetheless, of seventy-three senior staff members at Brookings, forty-nine had held at least one government post. During the Kennedy-Johnson years forty positions had been held by Brookings staff; during the Nixon years thirty-one positions had been held. The report seemed to allay some of the concerns. Still, a few trustees continued to voice doubts about staff members' policy positions being attributed to the institution. Joseph Pechman's pointed arguments for ending tax preferences were particularly nettlesome to some trustees. One even suggested that perhaps the time had come to drop standard disavowals about the scholars speaking for the institution and instead to assemble a board that fully agreed with the staff.[10]

By 1973, however, Gordon was beginning to wonder whether he might have overreacted to early White House criticisms, especially since working relations with executive agencies had never been a source of great difficulty. Even during the 1970s Brookings was offered many more federal research contracts than it could accept, and the conference programs for federal executives run by the institution's Advanced Study program were usually oversubscribed. Gordon noted the "cordial, fruitful, and trusting" relations with substantively oriented officials, but expressed some concern about "a residue of mistrust among the uninformed."[11] By 1975, with partisan tensions abating during the administration of Gerald Ford, Gordon reported comfortable and friendly relations with the White House and a much better understanding there of the institution's role. Nonetheless, Brookings would wear the journalistic tag line "liberal Democratic think tank" until well into the 1980s.

The End of Consensus

The nation's angry and corrosive divisions over the war in Vietnam shattered the broad consensus that had guided foreign policy since the end of World War II. The difficulties between members of the White House staff and Brookings were profoundly aggravated by differences over the war. Indeed, Kermit Gordon had seen the task of ending the war as the most urgent one facing the nation in 1968; others on the staff had worked vigorously for political candidates eager to extricate the United States from Vietnam. The relatively small elite that concerns itself with international affairs was badly fragmented by the war, and the lines of disagreement etched during the war would mark the contending factions for at least another twenty years.

The Brookings Foreign Policy Studies program had long been the smallest of its three research divisions. Given its origins and early staffing, it was arguably the most intimately involved in providing technical and administrative help to government agencies in the 1950s and 1960s. With the foreign policy consensus in disarray, Gordon turned his attention to expanding the program. In early 1969 he asked Henry Owen, who had headed the State Department's Policy Planning staff, to direct the program.

Rather than continuing primarily to prepare technical studies for the State Department, the Agency for International Development, or other executive agencies concerned with foreign policy, Gordon and Owen perceived realignments in the policy networks and new outlets for Brookings research. Senators, representatives, and their staffs had grown more assertive during the Vietnam years, but with few exceptions were relative newcomers to foreign policy deliberations. Washington-based journalists, long accustomed to following domestic issues, now found themselves covering intense debates about international matters. Business executives and their representatives in Washington were also more interested in monitoring American foreign policy.

When Owen assumed the directorship of the Foreign Policy Studies program, he outlined several assumptions that would shape the research. He predicted that the world's politico-military situation would be based on continuing strategic parity between the United States and the Soviet Union; he felt that the Europeans and Japanese would come to depend less and less on U.S. leadership; he thought that developing countries would achieve a degree of stability in the face of internal subversion; he foresaw increasing fragmentation in the communist world; and he believed that the industrial democracies would be inward looking, concerned primarily with their own domestic problems.

Three research areas emerged—national security, foreign economic policy, and northeast Asia. In the first, Owen wanted to ask what situations might require the use of U.S. force and what the capabilities and intentions of potential adversaries were. In the second, he continued to pursue Brookings long-standing interests in foreign aid while asking how economic relations among the industrial democracies might be improved. In the third, he sought to focus some of the institution's expertise on Asia, an area of growing importance and generally neglected by a policy elite long concerned with trans-Atlantic relations. The studies highest on his immediate agenda were those of the U.S. foreign aid role, a massive history of the World Bank, and the development of institutions for regional cooperation.

As always, changes in the program required new staff. Owen seemed to prefer to recruit people who had practical government experience rather than professors who did not, feeling that they had a surer grasp of what policy practitioners needed to know than did academic analysts. More broadly, Owen complained, "The problem is to find people who are not only original but good." Owens hired former State Department officials such as Edward Fried and Philip Trezise and William Kaufmann of Rand and the Defense Department to Brookings. He told Gordon that he also wanted to keep alert to recruit "smart odd-balls."[12]

Others on the staff also wanted to be sure that the organization was able to give a hearing to unconventional, nonestablishment views. Robert Asher expressed what he saw as some of the truths about hiring practices at Brookings. "In hiring people," he said, "we tend to look for those with the most impeccable credentials—i.e., names that will strike us, Kermit, the trustees, the government and the 'leading' eggheads as respectable, trustworthy, and capable of producing a competent piece of research. In judging whether the work is worth publishing, the important criteria tend to be balance, scholarship, lack of emotion, ideas that will impress but not distress 'the establishment.'"[13]

Owen sought out a cadre of younger analysts, most with government experience as well as reputations for novel thinking. Those he hired, including C. Fred Bergsten, Martin Binkin, Barry Blechman, Leslie Gelb, Morton Halperin, and John Newhouse, tended to bring economic and historical perspectives to bear on their work, breaking for the most part with the administrative concerns of their predecessors. He succeeded in assembling a group so independent in spirit that his relations with them were more than a little strained at times.

In 1969 Brookings initiated its Defense Analysis Project. The project represented the first attempt, completely independent of government funding, to assemble an analytic staff that could make unclassified quantitative analyses and projections about the long-term military posture of the United States and to link strategic questions with budgetary analyses. The project led to an annual analysis of the defense program and its financing, with volumes made available in sufficient time for Congress to use in its deliberations. The defense analysts have also contributed regularly to the *Setting National Priorities* series. During the 1970s the program of defense studies yielded brief volumes—a length deemed most likely to be read by Congress and the community of insiders—treating such topics as U.S. military reserve forces, the future of the marines, military pay, strategic bombers, prospects for naval arms control, the Soviet navy, and the U.S. force structure in NATO.

Another body of research began to look at Asia, where much of the work was in the hands of Ralph Clough and A. Doak Barnett. Clough was concerned primarily with defense issues and arms control in northeast Asia, while Barnett focused on U.S. diplomatic and economic relations with China as well as internal Chinese politics. The improvement in Sino-American relations that began in 1971 and the gradual strengthening of ties between the two nations brought attention especially to Barnett's work.

Born in Shanghai and educated at Yale, he had been a student in China during the revolutionary years of the late 1940s. After teaching at Columbia, Barnett joined Brookings in 1969 and produced several volumes on China during the 1970s. His 1971 volume, *A New U.S. Policy toward China,* addressed the issues that would have to be confronted before full diplomatic relations could be restored between the United States and China. His *Uncertain Passage: China's Transition to the Post-Mao Era* (1974), examined the forces that would shape the new leaders' quest for legitimacy and authority. He looked at civil-military relations, economic prospects, and ideological conflict in the wake of the Cultural Revolution, foreseeing the emergence of a generally pragmatic collective leadership that would push for more rapid economic development. Pragmatic economic reforms were not likely, however, to resolve questions about the relative roles of party, army, and bureaucracy. Although generally optimistic about a peaceful transition, Barnett did not rule out violent power struggles and unforeseeable shifts of power toward the military, revolutionary radicals, or provincial authorities.

Studies of foreign aid and international economic development had a long history at Brookings. Robert Asher reflected on the postwar American experience of foreign aid in a 1970 volume, *Development Assistance in the Seventies: Alternatives for the United States.* He found it ironic, given the nation's experience, that foreign aid should raise so much skepticism as an instrument of foreign policy. It had fostered economic growth, even if it had not always won political allies. He suggested ways of coordinating trade and investment policies with foreign aid as well as educational and scientific cooperation in order to make it still more effective in economic terms. To ease some of the political strains, he argued for placing more responsibility for aid in the hands of international organizations and for allowing developing countries to have a greater voice in determining the priorities for using the assistance.

The strengthening of international institutions—concerns that were paramount in the days of Moulton and Pasvolsky—persisted in the 1970s. Seyom Brown, in *New Forces in World Politics* (1974), explored the dynamics likely to shape world politics during the last quarter of the twentieth century. He predicted that nations of both East and West would have to confront domestic social, economic, and environmental problems, thus weakening the defensive alliances of the cold war. The Soviet Union especially would find it costly to postpone the day of reckoning with its economic problems, risking its control over Eastern Europe and its own dissident minorities. Brown argued that both the cold war coalitions and the nation-state were inadequate to manage global concerns. He urged all nations to build up the United Nations and other transnational organizations capable of resolving disputes. And he advocated more open markets in raw materials and greater financial aid for poor countries to encourage cooperation with the industrial nations in dealing with ecological issues.

Practical mechanisms for international discussions were also fostered by Brookings beginning in 1971 when it sponsored meetings in conjunction with experts from the European Community Institute for University Studies and the Japan Economic Research Center. The meetings led to short Tripartite Reports on a range of global issues in which Brookings published the analyses and recommendations of economists drawn from independent research institutions in Europe and Japan. Just as private research institutions had served as a mechanism for expert consensus to coalesce within the United States, the Tripartite meetings were designed to play a similar role across international boundaries.

Under Owen the Foreign Policy Studies program sought a wider audience for its research. Nonetheless, government agencies continued to turn to Brookings for help—the Arms Control and Disarmament Agency asked the institution to study Chinese nuclear capabilities, the Agency for International Development contracted for studies of public safety and technical assistance to developing countries, the State Department asked for a study of oceanic law. Private foundations, which had been somewhat circumspect about dealing with the Brookings Foreign Policy Studies program in the 1960s, once again provided support for the program, with Ford providing much of the funding for both the defense analyses and the studies of Asia.

As the postwar foreign policy consensus broke down, the institutional machinery of U.S. foreign policymaking was put to the test. Battles between the president and Congress over war powers, the oversight of the intelligence community, and arms control agreements underscored fundamental constitutional questions about American foreign policy-making. Several Brookings scholars were interested in the politics and institutional processes of making policy. Morton Halperin in his 1974 book, *Bureaucratic Politics and Foreign Policy,* asked what bureaucratic interests were at play within the U.S. government and then traced the interplay of information, argument, and public opinion as policies took shape and were implemented.

Leslie Gelb, who had directed the Defense Department's official history of Vietnam which came to be known as the Pentagon Papers, wrote *The Irony of Vietnam: The System Worked* (1979), with the assistance of Richard K. Betts. Using declassified government materials and presidential papers, the authors focused on how the policy system had functioned during the nation's most politically divisive foreign venture. They found that throughout the entire affair the system had responded to the sentiments of the majority. America did not stumble blindly into Vietnam; indeed, both the goal and the means were a result of the postwar consensus on the containment of communism. Moreover, policymakers knew from the outset that the war would be difficult and costly. In the final analysis, the policy results were disastrous, but the system had worked to produce a policy that responded to the convictions of the majority of Americans until public opinion finally and decisively turned against the war. The authors concluded that the lessons to be drawn did not concern the internal institutional processes but rather the interplay of dissent and disagreement.

Seeing Congress as an institution with the potential to scrutinize and check executive branch foreign policy initiatives, they were generally approving of the new congressional assertiveness in foreign policymaking. American policy on Vietnam had not somehow thwarted the majority's sentiments at the outset; rather the policy had not given an adequate initial hearing to dissenting and perhaps wiser views. Gelb and Betts were suspicious of doctrines that had become so ossified that they constrained choices and stifled debate; the authors concluded that sound policy is best shaped by contending centers of power and openness to dissent and disagreement.

In the years of dissent and confusion surrounding Vietnam, Watergate, and the economic crises of the early 1970s, Brookings came to be viewed as a center of opposition to Republican policies and a pillar of a liberal establishment composed of foundations, universities, the journalistic media, and publishing. The reality was far more complex. Although led by a man who had held high posts in Democratic administrations, the institution hired a number of Republicans and sought to keep the channels open to two successive Republican administrations. The labels, however, did not rub off easily even after the liberal establishment fell into disarray and liberalism as an intellectual force seemed to lose coherence and meaning.

7

SHIFTING CENTERS

AFTER A SIX-MONTH illness Kermit Gordon, not quite sixty years old, died in the summer of 1976. His work at Brookings was far from complete. Although never articulating a master plan, he built upon the financial and intellectual legacy of Robert Calkins. "Gordon presided with style, brilliance, and charm; he was a man of great presence," Henry Aaron recalled. "He was president when the stock market soared and we had no real competition. It was a period when it was easy to look good, and Gordon did it with style." Indeed, he had had the good fortune to arrive at Brookings just when applied policy research was flourishing within government and when university social scientists were easily drawn to the study of practical problems.

Gordon's principal talent lay in selecting strong program directors and bolstering their recruiting efforts by creating a genuine sense of intellectual excitement about the institution's role. His experience had taught him that tough-minded analysis could make a difference in policymaking—and Brookings would be the center for such work.

When Doak Barnett, the institution's China specialist, decided to leave Columbia University for Brookings, he cited Gordon's leadership as the lure. "I decided to come. If Kermit had not been president and the kind of person he was, I doubt I would have."[1] Other outstanding staff members were drawn to the institution for the same reason.

Gordon also earned a reputation for refusing to compromise on issues of quality. "If necessary a shorter list [of Brookings books] but a better one," he told his research directors. Like Calkins, he knew that long-term policy contributions depended on the intellectual rigor of the institution's work. The interplay with the academic community through the studies of economic regulation and the Brookings Panel on Economic Activity was fundamental in improving the practical analytic tools of social scientists. Gordon also had a gift for understanding how the social science disciplines interacted with one another. James MacGregor Burns, a colleague from Gordon's days at Williams College, remarked, "He knew where the disciplines of economics and political science joined and collided, where they supplemented and stimulated each other. Hence, if there is a science or even just an art of political economy, he embodied it."[2]

But Gordon's years at Brookings were marred by two realities. First, he had not entirely succeeded in erasing the perception of Brookings as partisan and liberal. Second, the institution's financial position had begun to deteriorate after the sharp stock market decline of 1973–74. The market value of the securities in the institution's endowment had fallen from a peak in 1972 of about $49 million to less than $33 million in 1976. While annual expenditures had remained in the vicinity of $7 million for five years, for three straight years expenditures had outrun revenues. The policy of drawing only 4.5 percent from its endowment for annual operating costs (the yearly amount is calculated on the endowment's three-year moving average) put the institution's ledgers in deficit by nearly $3 million in 1975 and nearly $2 million in 1976. The institution was not compelled to borrow money, but the deficits did cut into the endowment.

As the board members searched for a successor to Gordon it was clear that they wanted someone who could signal the institution's nonpartisan role. And even though Brookings had hardly drifted far from the political mainstream, the board wanted someone who could steer the institution toward a political center that was shifting to the right. The board also sought a strong financial manager. The institution needed someone who would wrestle with difficult budgetary decisions and seek out new sources of financial support to supplement the foundation resources that had been hard hit by declining financial markets and the inflationary surge of the early 1970s.

The board chose Bruce K. MacLaury, who took over from acting president Gilbert Steiner in early 1977. His candidacy had been strongly advocated by Robert Roosa, a long-time friend and associate with whom he had served in government and who had become chairman of the Brookings board in 1975. MacLaury, reflecting on his selection after a decade at Brookings, presumed he was chosen because he was viewed as "professionally nonpartisan." He arrived well briefed about the board's wishes to change the perception of the institution by nudging it toward the right, although MacLaury did not believe that he would have to push it very hard or far.

Like his three predecessors, he was trained in economics, having received a Ph.D. from Harvard University in 1961. Unlike Gordon, however, he was not strongly identified with either a particular party or administration despite a two-year stint as deputy under secretary of the treasury for monetary affairs during the Nixon administration. He had spent most of his career in the Federal Reserve, starting out as a research analyst with the Federal Reserve Bank of Boston and moving on to the Federal Reserve Bank of New York, where much of his work focused on international matters. On leaving the Treasury Department, he was appointed president of the Federal Reserve Bank of Minneapolis in 1971. Intellectually, he was drawn to the Brookings job because he admired the institution's books. "I had read Okun's *Equality and Efficiency*," he said, "and it was the framework for public policy that I believed in. That was the book that brought me here."

Questions of Money

Upon his arrival MacLaury found an institution in more serious financial difficulty than he had anticipated. He also entered a more complex and competitive environment in which to raise money than Gordon had experienced. Think tanks are fragile entities. And even with its endowment Brookings depends on a changing mix of funds drawn variously from foundations, corporate contributions, government contracts, individual donations, conference fees, and sales of publications.[3]

In the early 1970s Ford Foundation grants had accounted for about 30 percent of the institution's annual operating funds (earlier endowment contributions from the foundation further boosted the proportion of the Brookings budget derived from Ford sources to more than 40 percent in the early 1970s). Gordon, who had been a staff member at Ford and later served on its board, was able to maintain a relatively easy-going relationship between Ford and Brookings. Others at Brookings were also well regarded at Ford. "Pechman could raise seven figures with a two-page letter and a phone call," observed one staff member, no doubt with a touch of dramatic exaggeration as he reflected on easier financial times. On occasion, Ford officials even took the initiative, suggesting projects to the Brookings staff and occasionally serving as broker and funder of projects when a government agency needed help from an outside research group.

But the foundation was hard-pressed in the aftermath of the 1973–74 stock market decline. It made fewer long-term commitments to research projects, and for a time it sharply curtailed general support grants and capital gifts. By the late 1970s Ford sources accounted for only about 15 percent of Brookings operating income. The transition from heavy reliance on Ford to a more diverse funding base was not an easy one for Brookings. Later, in the 1980s, the Ford Foundation's insistence that grantees make continual, measurable progress in increasing the numbers of women and minority group members on their staffs occasionally strained relations between Brookings and its long-time funder.

The institution made up some of its losses in foundation support in the 1970s by taking on a larger share of government contract work, deriving nearly 20 percent of its funds from such contracts at the end of the decade, up from about 5 percent at the beginning of the 1970s. More than 20 percent of its revenues came from book sales and conference fees and just over 25 percent was provided by endowment earnings and other reserves. The rest of its operating income had to be raised annually from foundations, individuals, and corporations. The changing financial realities forced Brookings to ask some difficult questions about the sources of its income. What proportion of its funds could be derived from government sources without changing the character of the institution? How could it pursue corporate funding without jeopardizing the institution's independence? In what ways, since it had no alumni to appeal to, could it begin to solicit a greater share of its funds from individual donors? And how could Brookings build its endowment to insure against economic vicissitudes and to preserve intellectual autonomy?

Institutions that depend on money from outside sources are forever conscious of the taint that can arise, especially when their scholarship aspires to nonpartisanship, neutrality, and objectivity. Seeking to avoid appearances of bias and to insulate itself from vulnerability to donors' pressures, Brookings has had to establish explicit policies to govern the acceptance of money.

Policies about financial support, in fact, start with a clearly limited role for the trustees and a well-defined decisionmaking procedure in the research program. Decisions about new research initiatives should originate with the institution's scholars and conclude with rigorous outside academic review processes prior to publication. At Brookings the research must be on significant national policy issues; it must be limited to subjects within the areas of professional competence and interest of the staff and in line with the general research agenda set by the staff; it must be supervised by the institution, reviewed by professional peers, and dependent upon neither classified nor proprietary material; and ultimately the rights to publish must be retained by the institution.

Although an established structure for setting research agendas and reviewing projects is a beginning, it provides no guarantee that bias will not be perceived or alleged, especially when the institution tackles controversial policy issues. An institution must take additional steps to protect itself from exposure to financial pressures. Diverse support is the best protection, since susceptibility to pressure arises when funding is overly concentrated or highly volatile, or when an institution depends on only a few large projects. In the 1970s the trustees saw no problem in accepting as much as 15 percent of the total budget in federal money, but preferred not to rely on more. They knew that some projects, such as the Defense Analysis Project, should never be constrained by funding from defense agencies.

While acknowledging the risks and vulnerability of depending on outside funds, Brookings has always sought to raise as much general, long-term support as it can. It has set strict criteria for drawing on endowment income so that the margin of independence supplied by the endowment will not erode over time. By the late 1970s, with less general support coming from private foundations, Brookings began to look for new ways of increasing corporate support, a relatively untapped resource for Brookings at a time when corporate philanthropy was the fastest growing sector of American charitable giving.

MacLaury instituted several changes in trying to alleviate the institution's fiscal problems. First, he hired professional development officers and through a new Office of External Affairs began to build stronger links to the business community. The efforts paid off as corporate contributions rose from roughly $200,000 a year in the late 1970s to about $1.5 million annually by the mid-1980s. Second, the institution began to redefine the role of its board of trustees. Typically, when large foundation grants and endowment income provide most of the financial resources, a nonprofit institution does not need to rely heavily on its board as an engine for fund raising. Boards tend to be smaller, with college presidents, heads of nonprofit organizations, former public officials, and retired business executives dominating the membership. During MacLaury's tenure, the institution has sought to involve the board more directly in fund raising, expanding its size from roughly twenty-five members to about thirty-five, not counting the approximately twenty emeritus trustees who are also invited to meetings. The composition has also changed somewhat with still-active corporate chairmen and chief executive officers now serving in larger numbers. In these circumstances and during periods of straitened financial circumstance, board deliberations can also take on a different character. At Brookings questions of money and managerial direction moved inevitably to the fore in the late 1970s.

Brookings no longer occupied a unique and unrivaled position in Washington. The federal government's own capacities for research and analysis had expanded considerably over the years. The staffs of the 200-member Congressional Budget Office, the 140-member Office of Technology Assessment, the 900-member Congressional Research Service, and policy analysts working in various executive agencies were engaged in research no less proficient than the work done at Brookings. Other private think tanks, a few with budgets comparable to that of Brookings, had emerged in Washington by the early 1970s as well. They included conservative operations such as the American Enterprise Institute, which had been founded in 1943 and gradually built itself into a self-proclaimed "conservative Brookings," the Center for Strategic and International Studies, founded in 1962, and the Heritage Foundation, which enjoyed a meteoric rise after its founding in 1973. There were also solid, mainstream contract research organizations such as the Urban Institute, founded in 1969, and the Santa Monica–based Rand Corporation, which had been set up initially in 1945 as a research unit for the U.S. Air Force but had moved into domestic policy research during the early 1970s and had a sizable Washington operation. Narrowly specialized think tanks also emerged in the 1970s and 1980s.

By 1990 just over one hundred private think tanks were at work in Washington, giving shape to a complicated marketplace of ideas in which books, reports, and policy prescriptions were being aggressively promoted and sold. Comfortable assumptions about the role of research and, indeed, of ideas in public policymaking were being challenged.

Brookings, historically oriented toward the insider community of government experts and policy academics, did not move rapidly into this bustling public marketplace of ideas. It was not until the 1980 election, with the ensuing clamor of conservative think tanks celebrating their role in the Reagan revolution, that most observers even took note of the burgeoning ideas industry in Washington.[4]

Bruce MacLaury and his associates knew that they faced an increasingly competitive and ideologically charged intellectual environment, but promoting books and creating programs that would serve journalists or the wider public seemed out of keeping with the scholarly traditions of the institution. Only gradually and after debate that carried up to the board of trustees did Brookings begin to come to terms with the new environment and to reappraise its place in Washington. In 1981 the board approved several new strategies.

Books have been the primary Brookings product over the years. The institution has traditionally seen the book-length academic study as its principal instrument and the standard by which research projects are best judged. Books anchor the research program in projects that last for several years and consequently they give a certain intellectual continuity to the program. With roughly half of the book sales accounted for by college and university courses, books are also another means of linking the institution's research to the academic community. Through their books Brookings scholars are engaged, though indirectly, in university teaching.

Books have another function as well. Few people would argue that books have a direct impact on specific policy decisions. It is no secret that busy policymakers have little time to read and that they absorb information and analysis by many other means. Briefings, staff-prepared memoranda, casual conversations, op-ed pieces, book reviews, seminars, and conferences put ideas into play more readily than books. Books, however, are often the starting point for discussion, and indirectly they can redefine the framework within which policies are discussed. Perhaps more important, books are manifestations of expertise—they endow individual scholars and their institutions with an intellectual authority that can rarely be acquired by other means. Books are, as one Brookings scholar puts it, "a license to speak" on a given subject. And over the long term, they are a measure of an institution's commitment to advancing serious research rather than simply contributing ephemeral argument and passing commentary to public policy debates.

However, the financial exigencies of the early 1980s and the growing competition within the marketplace of policy books and reports compelled Brookings to ask questions about the nature of its publications. Scholarly research and the books that follow are almost always costly and time-consuming undertakings. Research institutions usually make their mark slowly (indeed, it is probably best that ideas move at a measured pace, allowing time for testing, deliberation, and persuasion). Nevertheless, both think tanks and their foundation sponsors sought more visible and immediate public impact for their dollar in the 1980s. They perceived stiffer competition in the policy book marketplace, where hundreds of books and reports vie for attention. In fact, some institutions seemed better geared toward producing more provocative and timely publications than Brookings, often targeting a particular ideological constituency. Some at Brookings felt that the institution needed to participate more visibly in the public arena, confronting more topical issues, underscoring policy recommendations, and accepting the fact that a book's ideas make their way in the policy process not simply by means of the bound and printed page but through talk, op-ed essays, popular reviews, and comment in the media.

In the early 1980s the institution began to produce shorter studies and to make greater efforts to extend the reach and impact of its research.[5] Staff members were expected to think about the topicality of the research projects they embarked upon and were urged to complete projects in a more timely fashion and under more realistic budgetary constraints. The emphasis on reaching a wider audience took several forms at Brookings. A somewhat staid research bulletin was replaced by the more marketable *Brookings Review* in 1982, which attained a circulation of 19,000 (with 4,000 paid subscribers) by 1990. A series of Dialogues on Public Policy (many of them emanating from the Center for Public Policy Education) started to appear in 1982, and short Task Force Reports with crisp recommendations were being issued as the 1980s came to an end.

Gilbert Steiner observed that the competition "has in very overt fashion changed the character of our product. There is less a disposition to produce complete analyses in book form, and a more pronounced disposition to comment in either testimony, short form, or very brief monographic form."[6] Brookings scholars did not overtly resist the changes; indeed, some thought the changes were overdue. Alice Rivlin, whose career included a term on the *Washington Post's* editorial board (to the bemusement and dismay of at least one of her senior colleagues who thought at the time that such journalistic labors were inappropriate for a serious scholar), said that she had "long been of an opinion that an institution that just writes books is not going to be as effective as one that also writes shorter things."[7]

Although some publications changed and scholars knew that they should take on a more visible public role, the underlying nature of the institution was not transformed in any decisive way. "We are never going to be mass communicators," said MacLaury. "We may get to be known more broadly, but we are still targeting leaders." The effort to target leaders more effectively led to changes in Brookings least understood operating division, the Advanced Study program, now its Center for Public Policy Education.

Dialogue and Leadership

The means of training and educating political leaders and citizens is an age-old problem. Great works of political theory, among them Plato's *Republic* and Machiavelli's *Prince,* have explored questions about education and the wielding of political power. In our own century we have taken much for granted about the relationship between educational and political institutions, placing most of our faith in the benefits of professional training and ever narrower specialization. As essential as such specialization may be in a complex society, it sometimes comes at the cost of producing leaders with a wide perspective, broad-ranging creativity, and, ultimately, political wisdom.

Brookings and the handful of research institutions founded in the early 1900s were part of this century's movement toward professional specialization. They sought to make political administration a more expert and scientific affair. Although its early experiment in formal graduate training and the awarding of degrees was short-lived, the institution's educational role continued through training and fellowship programs that have brought advanced graduate students to Washington. Brookings remains an active participant in the pursuit of more specialized knowledge about public issues. Its studies contribute to the slow accretion of the nation's intellectual capital.

In the mid-1950s Brookings embarked on a new educational experiment, one that has grown, in terms of revenues generated, into the institution's largest operating division. The Center for Public Policy Education (CPPE) is now directed by Lawrence J. Korb, an assistant secretary of defense in the Reagan administration. Korb, who directed defense policy research at the American Enterprise Institute, also holds a research appointment as senior fellow in the Brookings Foreign Policy Studies program.

The CPPE attracts less attention in academic circles than the institution's research-oriented endeavors. It has often resided a bit uneasily within Brookings, an institution that has devoted so much of its energies to research and publishing. At Brookings, as in leading research universities, the teaching function is often relegated to secondary status. And CPPE sometimes regards itself as an "intellectually poor cousin" of the research program, as one former member of the staff puts it. Nonetheless, the CPPE's educational programs have created countless informal bridges between the institution and federal executives as well as private sector leaders interested in public policy. "It is a fundamental way in which we are a part of Washington," observed Walter Beach, a senior staff member. "Thousands of people are able to say, I've participated in that, giving us an alumni network of sorts."

However, the center's stock in trade, dialogue and discussion, inevitably leaves fewer lasting intellectual marks than books and articles, even though the oral tradition may be more important to the practical conduct of politics among Washington's tribal communities than the written word. The CPPE's influence—like that of a general education—is even harder to trace than that of the scholarly book or research report. Barbara Littell, the center's associate director, speaks of the programs in broadly educational language; she describes the center as a place that offers its students perspective, tests and challenges their preconceptions, and seeks to integrate ideas.

The origins of the CPPE lay in an educational experiment in the mid-1950s, funded by the Ford Foundation and aimed at upper-level federal executives. Although the founders of Brookings were convinced that administrative competence was the starting point for good government, they probably would have been astounded to realize some forty years later that the growing professional specialization of civil servants could narrow their purview and inhibit their performance. No doubt, the founders would also have noticed that the old distinctions between the spheres of administration and politics, with separate competencies required in each, were becoming harder to maintain as government's scope widened. Thus, the program that took shape in 1957, with Robert Calkins serving as the driving force, was an exercise not in training executives in new managerial techniques but in political education in the widest sense. It lifted groups of twenty to thirty career officials out of their ordinary Washington settings and placed them in Colonial Williamsburg for seminars lasting from one to three weeks.

The early conference program, which brought together executives of the rank of GS-15 and higher with leading academics, ranged over works of philosophy, history, political theory, and sociology—from Alfred North Whitehead's *The Function of Reason* to David Riesman's *The Lonely Crowd*. Participants discussed such subjects as "The American Democracy" and "The Uses of Knowledge" as well as more discrete policy questions.

The experiment began with genuine doubt about whether federal executives would want to attend (some had to use accumulated vacation time to get away from their jobs), but the reception was enthusiastic. The reasons for the immediate and favorable response were not altogether clear. The conferences were kept small and the preferred method of teaching was Socratic dialogue. Yet typically the participants found it difficult to explain how the experience specifically enhanced "their competence or subsequent practice," as Robert Calkins conceded. More than thirty years after the initial experiment, Calkins still could recall an early participant who confessed that he had given up on serious reading (and perhaps on his career) until the conference programs recharged his intellectual enthusiasms and renewed his interest in government and politics.

One participant mused that asking about the program's specific value was "like asking what good it did to read *War and Peace*. When we try to pin it down to tangibles we tend to trivialize the concepts that this experience has given us."[8] Douglass Cater, another early observer of the program, remarked that "the intent is always to get away from specialities and to plow a deep furrow through the fields of general knowledge."[9]

The program acknowledged—as had the Hoover commissions of 1949 and 1954 which looked at government administration—that the Civil Service was no longer a "corps of clerks" and would benefit from some means of continuing both professional training and general education. The military had taken the lead in its career development programs through the National War College and Air University; business executives had the benefit of various corporate-run programs and the broader educational endeavors of such retreats as the Aspen Institute. Senior-level civil servants had nothing comparable.

Within two years the Brookings effort had spawned new training and educational programs in civilian agencies of government and, in part, had prompted the passage of the Federal Training Act of 1958 and the subsequent creation of the Federal Executive Institute. The experimental program—as a model fostering more permanent training programs—was a clear success. Having set other training activities in motion, Brookings staff members wondered whether their program needed to be continued. Despite the new government programs, the Civil Service Commission encouraged Brookings to continue its educational efforts. A new and larger Conference Program on Public Affairs was launched in 1959 and renamed the Advanced Study program in 1962. It was directed by James M. Mitchell, a former associate director of the National Science Foundation, who had also served as a Civil Service commissioner and a deputy assistant secretary of defense. He shaped the institution's youngest operating division, heading it until 1974.

The program expanded its reach into the private sector in 1961, finding a new constituency with a series of six-day programs to introduce senior business executives to the operations of the federal government and emerging policy issues. These Conferences on Understanding Federal Government Operations—UFGOs in Brookings argot—have been the mainstay of the public policy education program, attended by several hundred business executives a year. In 1964 Brookings began to bring together business executives and federal executives in one-day programs held around the country; and in subsequent years the program staff members have looked for other opportunities to span the boundaries separating business, government, professional, and labor leadership.

In 1970 a series of Round Tables on government, the economy, and American society served similar aims by focusing on the political environment in which business enterprises had to operate. Brookings found that it was not only the life-long civil servant who could benefit from such programs. In 1974 the institution organized policy seminars for members of Congress and congressional staff members under the general auspices of the Congressional Research Service of the Library of Congress; and in 1975 the institution began a series of meetings to orient newly elected members of the House and Senate.[10]

In time, individual government agencies assumed much of the cost of the programs for federal executives. For the most part, the Advanced Study program and the CPPE, its successor, have been sustained by the tuition fees its programs generate. By 1980 approximately five hundred federal executives were involved in conference programs each year, attending two-week-long general conferences on public policy issues, specialized programs for government science executives, conferences on business policy and operations, and shorter forums on critical policy issues. The essence of the program according to senior staff member Peter Malof was "to help the government executive, a specialist working in a vertical bureaucracy, to connect with other fields."

A program of adult education must always be in the process of reinventing itself. The Brookings program operates in a now well-developed marketplace of educational seminars and executive training programs, competing with schools of business and public policy, professional associations, in-house corporate training programs, and programs run for the business community by other think tanks. Often experimental programs will be taken over or copied by other organizations. When the President's Commission on Personnel Interchange, for example, set up a fellowship program in 1967, Brookings ended its Public Affairs fellowship program that had brought business leaders to Brookings to spend up to a year at the institution. Similarly, when the National Training and Development Service was set up, Brookings curtailed its programs for state and local leaders. And when the AFL-CIO set up its Labor Studies Center, Brookings found it difficult to attract union participants to its programs. Since the 1970s professional associations such as the American Bar Association and American Management Association have become competitors in offering policy-relevant conferences as well.

Walter Held, who succeeded James Mitchell as director of the Advanced Study program in 1974, viewed the program as a place for continuing experiments in "leadership education." As the program evolved, its offerings grew into an eclectic mix of topical conferences and courses on federal government operations. Held maintained that apart from the information participants acquired about particular issues and the technical and problem-solving skills they might enhance during a week or two of study, the program was an occasion for participants to reevaluate their preconceptions about policy issues and to bridge gaps in perception between government officials and leaders from other walks of life. Indeed, one of the underlying rationales for the Brookings program is its effort to bridge the divisions of a very fragmented policy system—divided by constitutional intent among executive, legislative, and judicial branches; further fragmented by the growth of modern bureaucratic structures; and complicated by the public-private dynamic of American policymaking.

Held and his successors in the Advanced Study program and the Center for Public Policy Education—James Carroll, A. Lee Fritschler, and Lawrence Korb—have emphasized the need for their programs in a society where public and private decisionmaking are not walled off from each other and where the movement of people from private to public sector and back is extremely fluid. In addition to its formal curriculum of fee-based and contract conferences and occasional public forums on particular policy issues, the Brookings Advanced Study program and the CPPE have provided a neutral ground where off-the-record, informal exchanges can take place among leaders who might not otherwise meet informally.

Beginning in 1978 Brookings provided just such a neutral terrain for officials concerned with the administration of justice. The chief justice, attorney general, and leading members of the House and Senate Judiciary Committees met in Colonial Williamsburg, and they or their representatives have continued to gather there annually.[11] The Brookings conferences have served as an informal, extra-constitutional arena designed to overcome the two-centuries-old constitutional barriers that have complicated the administration of the federal court system.

With Congress creating judgeships, setting salaries, and appropriating funds as well as holding the power to "ordain and establish" inferior courts, and with the executive branch holding considerable administrative authority, policymaking in this area is decidedly complex. The use of the courts by Congress to achieve substantive policy goals has added to the burdens of the judiciary. The administration of the judiciary, however, is seldom an item high on either branch's agenda. Moreover, judges and legislators approach the questions from different perspectives. Judges tend to see the advantages of having more judges in order to relieve the workload on the judicial system; representatives and senators tend to see the political ramifications of being able to make lifetime political appointments.

Historically, problems of administering the judiciary have been relegated to the margins, a matter of inertia and inattention. Recognizing that needed administrative reforms had sometimes been delayed for decades simply because the three branches had had no forum to discuss judicial problems, Warren Cikins of Brookings and Mark Cannon, administrative assistant to Chief Justice Warren Burger, set out to bring them together. Burger and Attorney General Griffin Bell were both keen on judicial modernization at a moment when congestion in the federal court system was propelling Congress toward a bill to expand the judiciary by some 150 judges. Although the Omnibus Judgeship Bill was already under discussion, the Williamsburg conference in 1978 served to educate many participants about the nature of the reforms, to reshape some provisions of the legislation, and to point the way for integrating a large group of new judges into the system.

Over the years the two-day or three-day conferences have allowed the principal policymakers (often joined by legal scholars) to meet and discuss issues ranging across court reorganization, procedure, judicial tenure and discipline, minor dispute resolution, sentencing, and other emerging issues. By the late 1980s roughly a dozen pieces of legislation affecting the judiciary had been born there.

The broad contours of the Advanced Study program were established early on, but in the late 1970s and early 1980s, program directors James Carroll and A. Lee Fritschler set in motion changes that led to the creation in 1985 of the Center for Public Policy Education. Carroll expressed concerns not only about the atomization of the Washington policy process but about the fragmentation of professional expertise. He saw a growing need "to overcome the limitations of professional and occupational specializations."[12] The pace at which new data and research findings moved ahead made it essential that the Brookings program work harder to synthesize and interpret research across professional boundaries.

His colleague Peter Malof shared the concerns about political fragmentation and conflict, arguing that in a modern political culture the flow of information binds the polity together. He has viewed the educational efforts of Brookings not as a classroom where knowledge is imparted from teacher to student but as an arena in which divergent perspectives are articulated. Even if disagreements are not resolved, the discussion can narrow the range of difference and foster respect among different constituencies.

The decision to rename and expand the Advanced Study program was driven by several practical concerns. Over the years, the reliance on fee-based and contract programs propelled the program toward routinized and recurrent offerings. The new Center for Public Policy Education would signify a renewed and expanded commitment to Brookings educational mission. The center would seek new sources of revenue and a broader constituency for its programs, one that would include journalists, leaders of nonprofit organizations, and professional groups. The new constituencies would require programs rather different from those that had introduced business leaders to the operations of government or helped government executives see their place in broader policy processes. The commitment to educational experimentation would necessarily be renewed as well. And as the institution was seeking larger audiences for its scholarly work, the new center would provide a public outlet for research. The new center was expected to resolve one of the most bedeviling problems in the educational program's twenty-five-year history by forging more systematic links to the scholars working in the three research programs. Finally, the center would also seek to organize international programs, hoping to build links with policy research groups and their constituencies in other countries.

Like Carroll, Fritschler saw CPPE as a mediating structure capable of bringing together diverse segments of American leadership. It was not a place for further academic study and research but for public dialogue. The "fragmentation of interests" in American life and the tendency to rely on adversarial processes had created what Fritschler termed a "confidence gap" among leadership groups. Noting how often Americans had turned to commissions to resolve policy quandaries, he thought that "extraordinary forums are needed, probably on a continuing basis." He argued, "The need for these forums is particularly acute on issues which broadly affect different communities and cannot be easily processed through the sub-system of government." He added that Brookings was an institution with sufficient stability and integrity to convene such "policy development" forums.[13]

The Center for Public Policy Education was formally dedicated in 1985. With such ambitious aims—communicating research to a wider audience, serving as a policy development forum, experimenting with educational technologies, expanding the international reach of the institution—it is hard to take a precise measure of the CPPE's work. Its mandate is large, its eight-member professional staff small given its tasks.

National issues forums have drawn audiences to hear Brookings scholars discuss their research findings; certainly, the center has helped expand journalistic coverage of the institution's research program. The center's international programs have also helped Brookings in its efforts to collaborate with research institutions and leadership groups in other nations. Bridge-building programs such as a labor-management seminar for United Auto Workers union officials and Ford Motor Company plant managers have shown the potential of Brookings as a neutral arena for mutual education; however, plans to duplicate the Administration of Justice seminars in other policy fields have met with mixed success. Specially designed programs for individual corporate and government clients have been held for executives from IBM, McDonnell Douglas, Exxon, the U.S. Navy, the Agriculture Department, and the Central Intelligence Agency, hinting at prospects for more "customized" educational programs. A collaborative program with a school of business, the Sloan School of Management at the Massachusetts Institute of Technology, has become a staple of the CPPE's efforts as well. Although the research program inevitably leads the way for the institution, the public policy educational program helps anchor Brookings in Washington's policy community and functions as a vital link to the business community as well. It serves the policy process, broadly conceived, by expanding the constituencies for sound policy research and fostering reasoned dialogue across intellectual boundaries, whether shaped by professional training, bureaucratic perspective, economic interest, geography, or nationality.

8

CONTINUITIES AND CHANGE

EXUBERANT REVOLUTIONARY rhetoric accompanied Ronald Reagan's electoral victory in 1980. Although national frustrations with inflation, disdain for big government, perceptions of impotence in the face of the hostage crisis in Iran, and fears of increased Soviet power had given impetus to Reagan's insurgent movement, the Reagan adherents spoke of a more deeply rooted intellectual revolution. They celebrated their victory as a triumph of ideas, referring not merely to programmatic ideas but to fundamental political ideals and values.

In the moment of conservative triumph, various commentators turned their attention to the tactics of a handful of think tanks that had apparently provided the conservative movement with its intellectual weaponry and personnel. Several of the institutions had pioneered in the production of short, timely, and well-targeted policy publications; they had proved exceedingly skillful in marketing policy proposals, elevating the public standing of their researchers, and keeping their institutions in the limelight as the places to which conservative policymakers turned for advice. Brookings, which had once served as a model for the conservative think tanks, acknowledged that it had something to learn from its rivals about reaching a wider audience.

Brookings in the Public Eye

Members of the press corps, better educated and working more specialized beats than ever before, are now a part of the nation's "issues networks." They are solidly welded to the capital's "iron triangles" of policy administrators, congressional staff members, and interest group lobbyists. And they are an important constituency to which policy research institutions must pay attention if books and research reports are to find a place in the public policy debate and if individual researchers are to gain the widest possible audience.

In 1981 Brookings hired its first public affairs director, Margaret Rhoades. For the first time, the institution began to think systematically about the media coverage of its studies, and it asked how the institution could respond to the demands of Washington's large journalistic corps. Brookings began to organize background briefings for the press before important presidential trips, economic summits, and arms control meetings. The institution made an effort to invite more journalists to conferences and seminars and on occasion arranged special briefing sessions for visiting foreign journalists.

While the institution obviously reaped benefits when its books were mentioned, its scholars quoted, or their op-ed essays placed in major newspapers, much of the work when journalists called—like the informal consultations with government officials—was to provide perspective and background. On an average day the public affairs department logs some twenty or thirty queries for Brookings scholars, while many more journalists each day are likely to call staff members directly. The release of a Brookings defense budget analysis or other timely volume can elicit as many as two hundred press inquiries.

This symbiotic relationship between research institutes and the Washington media is a complex phenomenon that serves simultaneously to elevate public debate and render it more confusing. There is now an almost ritualistic quality to the use of experts in both broadcast and print journalism; quotations from contending specialists serve as intellectual counterpoint in broadcast news segments and newspaper articles, lending a crude balance as well as intellectual authority to the reporters' efforts. At its best, reliance on think tank experts for background and perspective can raise the quality of reporting and make for more diverse and informed analysis. At its worst, it turns reporting into a pastiche of contending opinions without seriously evaluating the basis for the experts' claim to authority.

Relationships between journalists and scholars were brought into focus in a period of frenzied activity following Iraq's invasion of Kuwait in August 1990. The invasion awakened a somnolent Washington and aroused instantaneous journalistic interest in the work of experts who had been toiling for years in seemingly arcane fields.

Within hours of the invasion of Kuwait, the Brookings public affairs office was beseiged with some fifty requests for commentary and analysis. At the same time, some individual scholars already well known to specialized journalists fielded countless more calls on their own lines. The reporters were from large newspapers and weekly newsmagazines, network television news programs and public broadcasting, as well as local radio stations and small town newspapers scattered across the country. Their inquiries were sometimes narrowly focused on subjects such as the much-feared Iraqi chemical warfare capabilities, the mechanics of the presidential order freezing Iraqi assets, or the impact of lost Kuwaiti oil production. Sometimes the inquiries were more general, even desperate appeals for an expert who could speculate about the future or explain why events had unfolded as they had. Few Washington think tanks had assembled staffs with the breadth of interest of the complement of scholars at Brookings; indeed, the public affairs director of one of its rivals a few blocks away called in mid-morning to ask if he might refer reporters to Brookings since his own institute had run out of available experts.

Although William Quandt, a Brookings senior fellow who had served on the National Security Council staffs of Ford and Carter and written widely about the Middle East in books on Saudi Arabia, oil policy, and the Camp David accords, was away on vacation when the invasion began, a cluster of a half dozen scholars was quickly enlisted to respond to press inquiries. Judith Kipper, a Brookings guest scholar and consultant to ABC News, had been the first to be heard by the public, making a late-night appearance on "Nightline" as news of the Iraqi invasion broke. She remained busy the next day, averaging an interview every fifteen minutes. On the first full day of the crisis Thomas L. McNaugher, whose *Arms and Oil: U.S. Military Strategy in the Persian Gulf* had been published five years earlier, was called by some fifteen journalists before lunchtime; his day included interviews with *People* magazine and the *Army Times,* and an appearance on the "MacNeil/Lehrer NewsHour." Other scholars were almost as hard pressed, as journalists around the country scrambled to find people capable of offering insight and analysis.

Edward R. Fried, a senior fellow specializing in trade policy, was asked for his assessment of oil problems. Ralph C. Bryant, a senior fellow who had written on international finance, was queried about the assets freeze. Joshua M. Epstein, a senior fellow and author of *Strategy and Force Planning: The Case of the Persian Gulf* (1987) as well as a defense budget analyst, dealt with reporters perplexed about the military options. Yahya M. Sadowski, a research associate specializing in the Middle East and terrorism, fielded calls from nearly a dozen journalists on the first day when war seemed to be imminent. Elisa D. Harris, a senior research analyst, emerged on the networks as the most publicly visible expert on chemical and biological warfare. Lawrence Korb, in Aspen when the invasion began, handled press calls from the outset and, early in the crisis, drafted an op-ed piece that set out widely used figures on what the American military response would cost; he also suggested how the costs could be met without jeopardizing the post–cold war peace-dividend.

As the United States encountered its first major crisis in the post–cold war era, many other Brookings scholars were called upon in ways that reveal both the range of the institution's long-term research program and the overt public role that experts are called upon to play in our society. Specialized policy experts no longer serve merely as advisers in the shadowed alcoves of power. Instead, they are now expected to operate under the glare of television lights, their opinions and insights available to large audiences. At times, events give an urgency to their work that is very different from the more measured pace of scholarly analysis.

In dealing with the press, Brookings scholars will grumble about the demands on their time and the unexpected, always insistently urgent interruptions to their research and writing; some estimate that between 20 and 40 percent of their time is spent dealing with the press. Occasionally they will complain about interviewers fishing for a pre-determined viewpoint to round out a story or to add the analytic gloss of an expert's authoritative phrase or sentence. Nevertheless, most see their relations with the press as part of their professional duties, an educational responsiblity and a public service obligation. In immeasur-able but very real ways, their responsiveness to press inquiries can help shape the analysis of contemporary events and gradually enlighten that segment of the public which is attentive to the news.

New Directions in Politics

The conservative ascendance in Washington—and the new policy directions suggested in the agenda-setting volumes emanating from the

Heritage Foundation, the Hoover Institution, the American Enterprise Institute, and other conservative think tanks in 1980—promised decisive breaks with the policy continuities of the New Deal and the Great Society. At the top of the new president's political agenda were plans for tax and budget cuts grounded in supply-side economics and a large increase in military spending.

Scholars at Brookings also set out their agenda as the decade opened. Ten years after the first volume in the *Setting National Priorities* series, Joseph Pechman edited a volume subtitled *Agenda for the 1980s*. Instead of focusing on the president's budget, as past volumes had, the new book examined the broader domestic and international issues that Americans would confront in the new decade. The Brookings authors were troubled by many of the same problems that concerned the Reagan revolutionaries—energy policy, social and environmental regulation, Soviet expansionism, and confrontation in the Persian Gulf. Among the various essays those by Barry P. Bosworth and William Kaufmann pointed to ways in which the Brookings research program diverged from the agenda pursued by the new president.

Bosworth, who had directed President Carter's Council on Wage and Price Stability from 1977 to 1979 and then returned to Brookings to resume his position as senior fellow, confronted the central issue of the era, exploring the inflationary dynamic that had plagued the nation since the late 1960s. Because the causes of inflation did not lie primarily in excessive aggregate demand, the cures were not to be found exclusively in traditional fiscal and monetary remedies. A mild recession would not break the pent-up pressures; a long and harsh recession, its outcome uncertain, might not be worth the human toll. Inflation, he argued, was linked to long-term problems such as falling productivity growth, capacity shortages in some industries, and rates of capital formation that had not matched the expansion of the nation's labor force—all were problems that would continue to drive Brookings research during the 1980s. Bosworth's analysis as the decade began produced no one-shot solutions such as those propounded by the supply siders. Instead, he offered a series of measures focusing on fiscal restraint, an easier monetary policy, oil import restrictions, discrete measures to stabilize grain and housing prices, and tax incentives to promote investment, especially in research and development.

More tentatively, he suggested that an incomes policy might be necessary and certainly preferable to a severe recession. Bosworth warned, however, that policymakers had consistently underestimated the magnitude of the nation's economic problems; and in relying on half-hearted, gradualist policy measures, they had contributed to public disillusionment with government. The political debate had so far offered only painless remedies, misleading the public about the nature and ultimate costs of breaking inflation, while avoiding all talk of how those costs would be allocated.

William Kaufmann's essay sounded a theme that would be central to much of the institution's analytic work in the field of national security. With many policy analysts convinced that Soviet military spending had proceeded at a pace and level far surpassing Western expenditures, the debate on American nuclear forces had moved to the fore in the 1970s. Kaufmann, echoing controversies that had raged twenty years earlier, argued that nonnuclear forces also needed to be modernized and improved. He contended that nuclear forces in both countries were diverse and roughly equal and that each nation could survive long enough so that neither side had an exploitable strategic advantage. But he argued that the modernization of U.S. nuclear forces—the plans for a mobile land-based missile (MX) and the larger and more accurate missile (Trident II) for its submarines—should not lead to neglect of conventional forces. Kaufmann advocated a conventional force structure that could simultaneously meet attacks in the Persian Gulf, reinforce Western Europe, and answer military challenges in the Pacific or Caribbean. Seeing a growing and more varied threat from the Soviet Union in the wake of the invasion of

Afghanistan and with revolutionary ferment elsewhere, Kaufmann called for significant real increases in military spending above the Carter administration's plans, but he urged that most of the increase be devoted to conventional forces.

During the 1980s scholars in the Governmental Studies program posed questions about the Reagan revolution that they had often asked about American politics. They continued to look at such issues as political realignment, the role of parties, interbranch deadlock, and federal-state relations. Martha Derthick, who had taken over from James Sundquist as director of the Governmental Studies program in 1978, explained that the driving question at Brookings had always been "What works?" However, when it was formulated as an instrumental question about political institutions and processes, Derthick conceded that questions about workable means had not left much leeway at Brookings for examining the ethical and moral dimensions of policy. In focusing on the means and instruments of policy, Brookings scholars had seldom concerned themselves explicitly with the role of ideology, ideas, and values in politics. The Reagan years suggested that processes were being driven by ideas, and some Brookings scholars turned to those broad questions.[1]

A. James Reichley had begun to explore the conservative resurgence in the late 1970s, publishing *Conservatives in an Age of Change: The Nixon and Ford Administrations* in 1981. In a nation that had long dismissed the role of ideology (or that had found such wide agreement within the liberal tradition that ideological disputes seemed to matter very little), Reichley asked what effect ideology had had on policymaking in the 1970s. He looked at the force of conservative ideology during the Nixon and Ford administrations, reviewing both the cluster of ideas that define American conservatism and the political groupings that make up the Republican party. Reichley, a former legislative secretary to Republican governor William Scranton of Pennsylvania and a consultant to the Ford administration, distinguished "positional" conservatives, who are concerned about social order and approach social change cautiously, from "ideational" conservatives, who view themselves as custodians of Western traditions and seek a more radical restoration of fundamental values.

Seeing the apparent exhaustion of liberal and socialist ideologies as the decade began, Reichley thought it possible that ideational conservatism would experience an "enduring resurgence," but only if it avoided becoming "a rationalization for organized greed" or "a soapbox for belligerent nationalism." He challenged conservatives to build a political philosophy that would reflect "the aspirations of the human spirit, as well as the hard-won lessons taught by experience about the limits imposed by the human condition."[2]

The politico-religious revivalism of the 1970s, a political Great Awakening that was part and parcel of the conservative resurgence, prompted Reichley to write *Religion in American Public Life* (1985), a reconsideration of the religious issue in this country. The work marked a departure in some respects from conventionally defined Brookings policy books. But with the strong backing of Bruce MacLaury, who persuaded the board that the book was important for understanding the dynamics of contemporary politics, Reichley set out to study the historic relationship between religion and government from the time of the founding.

Reichley argued that freedom in American society "depends ultimately on religious values for cohesion and vindication of human rights." Secular value systems, rooted either in the individualism of the British utilitarians or the communitarian traditions of Rousseau, Hegel, and Marx, are an inadequate foundation for American civic life. From the struggle for American independence to the abolitionist cause to Progressive Era reforms, religion played a powerful role in American life. Reichley reviewed the constitutional interpretation of the establishment and free exercise clauses of the First Amendment, asking how institutional separation can be preserved while acknowledging that religion has a valuable part to play in the affairs of the nation. Reichley ventured a strong warning: while churches must denounce social evils and take stands on issues of principle, they must avoid becoming partisan combatants and getting involved in the hurly-burly of politics. Churches can act as mediators and fact finders on many issues, but to do so they must cultivate reputations for open-mindedness about political means. Nurturing moral values and humanizing both capitalism and democracy are roles that the church cannot play as a partisan combatant. Nor should churches too often test the limits of public tolerance of their role. Reichley's book on religion stood as an imminent warning against the rigidity and dogmatism that religious institutions can bring to political discourse.

James Sundquist continued his work on American political institutions. His *Decline and Resurgence of Congress* (1981) signaled one of the principal themes of the institution's political analysis in the 1980s—the problems arising from "divided government." Sundquist reviewed the political history of the relationship between the president and Congress. He recounted the decline of congressional power through the early 1970s, the confrontations with Nixon, and the reassertion of power through budget legislation, war powers, the legislative veto, and legislative oversight. Although the book looked back over the preceding decade, it hinted at the deadlock of the 1980s and the increasing dissatisfaction surrounding Congress. Sundquist explained how limited the congressional capacity for political leadership and policy integration is. Asking why Congress cannot be more coherent in setting a policy course, he answered that the national interest cannot be calculated by simply summing the interests of 535 members, each of whom feels the pull of individual constituencies. In an institution grounded in the principle of representation with its inherently individualistic traits, political rewards tend to flow to those who pursue parochial interests;

in addition, it became abundantly clear by the end of the decade that the House and Senate were structured in ways that invited the membership to evade political responsibility.

The fundamental disabilities of the political system would propel other Brookings studies by the end of the 1980s. Sundquist took perhaps the broadest view of the underlying dissatisfaction with the political system in *Constitutional Reform and Effective Government* (1986). The problems of the American constitutional system have brought periodic calls for fundamental reform. The calls seemed to grow more numerous as a system of checks and balances and divided government engineered in the 1780s approached its two-hundredth anniversary. But despite many proposals for reform over the years, only two of the twenty-six amendments to the Constitution had actually altered political arrangements—the seventeenth providing for the direct election of senators and the twenty-second limiting the president to two terms. The problem of political stalemate worried so many people that at least a dozen reform proposals were in the air during the 1980s. Sundquist considered the reforms intended to remedy the executive-legislative impasse: team tickets, lengthened terms of office for senators and representatives, limited-item vetoes, and national referenda, among others. Despite setting out an ideal series of amendments, in the end Sundquist chose to acknowledge the political realities. As bad as governmental indecision and stalemate seemed, the nation's affairs were not in peril and constitutional reforms had not yet stirred up a popular movement (or even won much elite support). Given the hurdles of the amendment process, constitutional reform seemed unlikely.

The Washington press corps had swollen in size and importance during the 1960s and 1970s, roughly doubling between 1950 and 1980. The metaphorical Fourth Estate had grown into an informal Fourth Branch of the Washington power structure, and its members were sometimes deeply embroiled in the political events they covered.

Accusations of partisanship and ideological bias had often been made, reaching a crescendo during the Watergate investigations. Stephen Hess turned his attention from presidential campaigns and White House organization to the culture of political journalism, producing several books in a series called Newswork. His first volume, *The Washington Reporters* (1981), was based on interviews and surveys of more than half the 1,250 reporters covering Washington. Far from finding reporters as a group committed to social activism or embarked on political crusades, he concluded that most were drawn to Washington not by their political ideals but by the simple opportunity to witness the national political drama and to work in proximity to politically powerful figures. The stereotype of a crusading liberal press corps, perhaps accurately descriptive of an earlier generation (and part of the media's own mythology about itself), seemed outmoded to Hess, who found reporters increasingly conservative and apolitical. He also looked skeptically at their working methods, finding that they focused on elected officials rather than agencies and bureaus. His research also found that few stories ever drew on research or close reading of documentary records. Instead, reporters relied primarily on interviews and press briefings.

Two subsequent volumes, *The Government/Press Connection: Press Officers and Their Offices* (1984) and *The Ultimate Insiders: U.S. Senators in the National Media* (1986), explored the interplay between public officials and the press. Hess's work was an answer to diverse press critics, both those who found journalists too powerful and those who found the press too complacent. Hess argued that the press in its symbiotic relationship with officials tends to affirm the power of those who already hold it.

Throughout the 1980s, when institutional deadlock and other obstacles to political action were widely evident, a number of projects examined the underlying dynamics of policymaking in discrete policy areas. The politics of policymaking remained a principal theme of research in Governmental Studies. Gilbert Steiner wrote on the futility of family policy, the stalemate over the equal rights amendment, and abortion, the most intractable and bitter domestic dispute of the decade. Robert Katzmann wrote on the politics of disability and the shaping of U.S. transportation policy. Martha Derthick and Paul J. Quirk collaborated on a study underlying the movement for deregulation. Derthick also collaborated with Paul Quirk in a study of the politics underlying the movement for deregulation. Studies by R. Kent Weaver of the politics of railway policy and of the indexation of government benefits took a similar analytic tack, as did Pietro S. Nivola's study of energy conservation, Lawrence D. Brown's study of health maintenance organizations, and R. Shep Melnick's study of the court's role in applying the Clean Air Act.

When focused on discrete policy areas, the work of the Governmental Studies program seldom argued for sweeping policy changes. The program reflected a realism about political and institutional deadlock as well as a healthy skepticism about the impact of reform measures in any well-trod policy area. Derthick, noting that "the truly important issues of public policy do not die," argued that the "more important they are, the less susceptible they are to decisive solutions or to the recommendations of 'quick and dirty' reports."[3] She and her successors—Paul Peterson, a political scientist from the University of Chicago who headed the program from 1983 to 1987, and Thomas Mann, former executive director of the American Political Science Association who assumed the directorship in 1987—were political scientists studying an often deadlocked institutional process. They found it difficult to be concerned with policy outcomes when policy change seemed so unlikely to come about in most areas. Moreover, as Peterson put it, "Something about the nature of our topics makes us reluctant to come up with a blueprint for reform. Description is more important than prescription in this [research] division." Mann echoes the sentiments of his predeces-

The work of Brookings scholars evokes some inventive images from political cartoonists.

Kermit Gordon, after teaching at Williams College and serving as a member of the Council of Economic Advisers and director of the Bureau of the Budget, was president of Brookings from 1967 until his death in 1976.

Bruce K. MacLaury, former deputy under secretary of the treasury and former president of the Federal Reserve Board of Minneapolis, has been president of Brookings since 1977.

Henry Owen served as director of the Foreign Policy Studies program from 1969 to 1977.

Gilbert Y. Steiner directed the Governmental Studies program from 1967 to 1976 and was acting president of Brookings in 1976–77.

Arthur M. Okun taught at Yale and served on the Council of Economic Advisers before coming to Brookings in 1969.

Joseph Pechman headed the Brookings Government Finance program from 1960 until his death in 1989. He directed Economic Studies from 1962 to 1983.

James L. Sundquist has been associated with Brookings since 1965 and directed the Governmental Studies program from 1976 to 1978.

Paul Peterson, director of Governmental Studies from 1983 to 1987, taught at Harvard, the University of Chicago, and Johns Hopkins University.

Martha Derthick, director of Governmental Studies from 1978 to 1983, has written about social security policymaking and regulation.

Thomas Mann, former executive director of the American Political Science Association, has directed Governmental Studies since 1987.

John Steinbruner, who has written on nuclear strategy, international alliances, and political decisionmaking, has led Foreign Policy Studies since 1978.

After eight years as director of the Congressional Budget Office, Alice M. Rivlin returned to Brookings in 1983 and directed Economic Studies until 1987.

Director of Economic Studies from 1987 to 1990, Charles L. Schultze has been affiliated with Brookings since 1968. He directed the Bureau of the Budget from 1965 to 1967 and was chairman of the Council of Economic Advisers from 1977 to 1980.

Henry Aaron, a senior fellow since 1968 and former assistant secretary of Health, Education, and Welfare, became director of Economic Studies in 1990.

James D. Carroll widened the perspectives of government and business executives as director of the Advanced Study program from 1979 to 1981.

A. Lee Fritschler directed the Advanced Study program and its successor, the Center for Public Policy Education, from 1981 to 1987.

Lawrence J. Korb, a former assistant secretary of defense, became the director of the Center for Public Policy Education in 1987.

The conferences on the administration of justice have brought together members of all three branches of government to discuss judicial reform. On this occasion those in attendance included Chief Justice William Rehnquist and Attorney General Edwin Meese III.

The Friday lunch is a Brookings tradition where policymakers and scholars meet informally.

sors: "Our broad objective is to describe, explain, and evaluate national political institutions and policy processes, to recommend changes in governing structures, and to formulate political strategies for working around constraints on effective government."[4]

One book that did prescribe a course of bold policy action was John E. Chubb and Terry M. Moe's study of school reform, *Politics, Markets, and America's Schools* (1990). They advocated a system of market competition and incentives to break the bureaucratic rigidities impeding school reform. Both the trenchancy of the policy argument and the fact that the proposals, similar to those advocated by conservatives and libertarians, had been set forth by scholars affiliated with the Brookings Institution provoked wide comment.

While scholars in Governmental Studies continued to ask, "What works?" by the end of the 1980s they were directing this question not only at specific policies but also at the broad framework of American institutions. Some posed the question, "Can the government govern?" Divided government was so fully institutionalized that virtually all questions of policy formulation and implementation had been subordinated to the executive-congressional struggle. Much of the work under way—Joel Aberbach and Christopher H. Foreman, Jr., on congressional oversight, Mann and colleagues on foreign policymaking, Robert A. Katzmann on Congress and the courts, Pietro Nivola on the politics of foreign trade regulation, Charles O. Jones on presidential mandates and governance, Kent Weaver on income transfer programs—was motivated by the effort to understand institutional incapacities.

As members of the Governmental Studies program looked toward a research agenda for the 1990s, they were grappling with perhaps the most serious institutional disability of our system—the apparent mismatch between the long-term nature of the nation's most intractable problems and the truncated perspective of its political leaders and citizenry. Brookings scholars, long concerned with policy effectiveness, administrative competence, and institutional capacities, were compelled to ask questions about the essential competence of the American polity, its ability to define distant goals, make difficult choices among means, elicit civic support for policy objectives, and act consistently over the long term.

9 SETTING NEW AGENDAS

WHEN ALICE RIVLIN took over the directorship of the Economic Studies program from Joseph Pechman in 1983, she ventured some thoughts on the contemporary climate for economic research in the United States. Much of what passed for research in the 1980s, she contended, was either "shoddy and ideological or elegant, irrelevant" work.[1] At Brookings where there were, as she put it, "no extremists, no single-answer people," the program hewed to the pragmatic center, while the nation's policy discussions often veered toward extremes.

As budget and trade deficits worsened during the 1980s, political debate either set off in search of panaceas or was afflicted by political stasis, especially when it came to dealing with the budget deficit. Charles Schultze saw it as an "aberrational period," one in which ideologues on both sides had a greater impact on policy debate than they deserved. "I think you can get rational dialogue," he observed in 1986, "but only if you can start from the right base line of a $50 billion deficit. The last fifteen years in the economy and the last five in the budget were aberrations."

The Economists' Priorities

Throughout the 1980s the budget process seemed less able to serve as an arena for setting priorities and shaping broad economic policy. It had turned instead into an outright political contest over cutting or preserving programs. By 1983 the *Setting National Priorities* series, whether it focused on the president's budget or broader policy choices, seemed irrelevant to a debate fixated on budget cutting. In 1984, when Brookings initiated a successor series, *Economic Choices*, its message that taxes would inevitably have to be raised resonated nowhere (except perhaps in Walter Mondale's failed bid for the presidency).

The policy departures of the Reagan administration altered the contours of public policy debate. Not only did the rhetoric and symbolism differ, so did the range of options that could be placed on the national agenda. The Brookings Economic Studies program shifted some research emphases as the national agenda changed, but it also pushed ahead with its traditional lines of research on macroeconomic policy, regulation, international economics, regulation, and productivity.

Work in social economics and social policy more broadly conceived continued, though at a diminished level. Louise Russell produced studies of preventive medicine and the medicare payment system. Henry Aaron and William B. Schwartz examined medical costs. Alicia Munnell continued her work on retirement policy, although shifting her focus from social security to the study of private pensions. Anthony Downs and his colleagues began to look at the causes of urban decline, seeking discrete diagnoses for the woes in individual cities.

The institution's pioneering work on economic growth continued unabated. Edward F. Denison persisted in analyzing the ingredients of economic growth, looking for explanations of the slowdown that began in 1974. His *Accounting for Slower Economic Growth: The U.S. in the 1970s* (1979) pointed to inflation, regulation, energy prices, taxes, and lower research and development spending as the underlying causes, although he found the impact of each small and unmeasurable. His *Trends in American Economic Growth, 1929–82* (1985) and *Estimates of Productivity Change by Industry: An Evaluation and an Alternative* (1989) further refined his analyses of the sources of productivity growth and its decline.

The advent of the Reagan administration, whose supply-side advocates had advanced sweeping claims about the relationship between taxes and individual economic effort, propelled tax policy questions to the fore. The work of Brookings on government finance took on new significance as it looked at tax alternatives. Henry Aaron and various colleagues edited volumes on the value-added tax, hybrid income-consumption taxes, social security financing, and the prospects for tax reform. With Michael Boskin, Aaron edited a volume on the economics of taxation to commemorate the twentieth anniversary of the government finance program.

In the late 1970s Joseph Pechman and Joseph Minarik had worked on the problem of the distribution of the tax burden in the United States. Compiling computerized data files on household income, consumption, and employment and demographic data from 1960 to 1978 (derived from the Census Bureau and the Internal Revenue Service), they built on the earlier study by Pechman and Benjamin A. Okner, *Who Bears the Tax Burden?* (1974). Pechman in *Who Paid the Taxes, 1966–85?* (1985) found that the tax burden had gradually grown less progressive. Analyzing the data under several different sets of assumptions, he found the system either moderately progressive or slightly regressive (the difference depending on what assumptions were made about whether the burden of corporation income taxes and property taxes are ultimately passed on to consumers).

Aaron and Pechman in *How Taxes Affect Economic Behavior* (1981) analyzed competing claims about tax effects on labor supply, business investment, corporate finance, stocks, capital gains, housing, savings, and charity. They concluded that taxes affected these things but never so much as the supply siders claimed.

Barry Bosworth in *Tax Incentives and Economic Growth* (1984) also put the arguments of supply-side economists to the test. He argued that while tax policies can affect savings, investment, and work effort, the 1981 tax cut failed to link tax incentives with other policies designed to spur economic growth. He examined the complexity of capital formation in an environment where private saving could increase but the national saving rate would decrease because of growing government deficits, which constitutes negative savings; he pointed to the variations in tax rates on different types of capital and the consequences for capital formation; and he suggested that shifting the tax burden from capital to wage income would discourage the work effort the supply siders had hoped to encourage and upon which the success of their theories was predicated.

One of the milestones of the Reagan administration was the Tax Reform Act of 1986. Political credit for the comprehensive tax reform legislation was widely—and deservedly—shared, from President Ronald Reagan and Treasury Secretary James Baker to Senators Bill Bradley and Robert Packwood of the Senate Finance Committee. Intellectual credit could also be apportioned across party and ideological lines, from supply siders arguing for lower marginal rates to liberals arguing for the closing of loopholes and an end to tax preferences. As financial journalists and editorial writers appraised the legislation, many of them paid intellectual tribute to Pechman and the work he had done in the Brookings Government Finance program for more than a quarter century.[2] The policy result had not come quickly, nor could Pechman as an economist nor Brookings as an institution have singlehandedly brought it about by sheer force of intellectual argument. Nevertheless, the body of research had gradually helped elite opinion coalesce around a broad goal of broadening the tax base and lowering rates.

A number of Brookings studies in the 1980s explored the interrelationships of the world economy, seeking to strengthen international economic institutions, to encourage a regime of freer trade, and to understand how macroeconomic policies in various nations interacted. During the 1980s Ralph C. Bryant wrote and edited five volumes on international monetary policy, international financial interdependence, the U.S. international payments deficit, and macroeconomics in an interdependent world.

The balance-of-payments deficit, which had grown suddenly and dramatically in the 1980s, aroused the most anxiety, fueling protectionist sentiments and calls for severe fiscal restraint from critics of U.S. policy at home and abroad. Bryant's work on the balance of payments found no great mystery in the causes of the U.S. external deficit—the reasons were principally macroeconomic. Solutions would require a careful international coordination of macroeconomic policies, since measures to reduce the U.S. budget deficit alone would have a deflationary effect on economic activity outside the United States. The macroeconomic interactions spurred Brookings to collaborate with the Centre for Economic Policy Research in London in a research project examining macroeconomic interactions and policy design in interdependent economies.

Robert Z. Lawrence also addressed trade issues in *Can America Compete?* (1984) and *Saving Free Trade: A Pragmatic Approach* (1986), which he wrote with Robert Litan. Lawrence challenged prevalent assumptions about the decline of the manufacturing sector and its debility in the face of international competition. Manufacturing employment during the 1970s increased more rapidly in the United States than in any other country and its productivity levels remained the highest in the world. Moreover, a long-term postwar decline in the U.S. share of world trade in manufactured goods had been arrested. An opponent of selective industrial policies, like most of his Brookings colleagues, he nonetheless advocated government funding for basic research and development. He also advocated government loan programs to finance the training and education of workers. On the whole, he concluded that a better-balanced set of macroeconomic policies could dramatically improve American trade competitiveness.

Regulatory studies continued on two fronts with general examinations of social and environmental regulation and detailed studies of the impact of regulation in particular industries. Lester B. Lave and Gilbert S. Omenn challenged the conventional wisdom about the impact of the 1970 Clean Air Act in *Clearing the Air: Reforming the Clean Air Act* (1981). While the act's regulations on new industrial plants and new cars had indeed prevented some environmental deterioration, they argued that many improvements in air quality had resulted from changes antedating the legislation, including the substitution of oil and natural gas for coal. Moreover, they found the act to have been poorly and ineffectively implemented. The authors urged Congress to clarify the federal-state roles and to update air quality standards in response to scientific knowledge about particular pollutants and levels of risk. They also proposed a range of economically based emission control strategies to modify a rigid legalistic structure of regulation.

Lave, who had worked with Carter administration officials in efforts to amend the Progressive-Era Food and Drug Act of 1906, also wrote and edited volumes on theoretical and scientific aspects of social regulation. Much of the Brookings work advanced arguments for what Lave described as "a middle course between complete reliance on market regulation through caveat emptor and government control of design and production."[3] With practical insight into the huge burdens of administering and enforcing a regulatory regime, Lave and his colleagues argued that scientific research, cost-benefit analysis, and risk assessment should all be better integrated into regulatory decisionmaking. Regulations, they concluded, had to be based on clearly set priorities rather than on vaguely defined social goals. The information resulting from better data collection and analysis also had to be used so that decisionmakers beyond the environs of regulatory agencies would be enlisted in the pursuit of widely shared social and environmental objectives.

The work on regulation during the 1980s brought to Brookings a cluster of scholars interested in specific industries and in microeconomics. Robert Crandall, for one, produced books on the future of the steel industry and the control of industrial pollution; he and several collaborators also looked at the regulation of the automobile industry. Other young economists joined the staff and began to assess the impact of the movement toward deregulation in the 1970s.

Steven Morrison and Clifford Winston published *The Economic Effects of Airline Deregulation* (1986). Eight years after the Airline Deregulation Act of 1978 they concluded that lower fares and better service had saved travelers $6.0 billion and improved airline earnings by $2.5 billion. They found that business travelers had especially benefited from the hub-and-spoke operations under which airlines were organizing their operations. As yet, they found no discernible losses of service in small communities or adverse effects on industry employment, although they did notice the first signs of two-tier wage structures in which newly hired workers were paid much less than older employees, which hinted at adverse long-term effects on labor. Foreseeing even greater gains in airline efficiency as competition worked upon the industry, the authors predicted that even takeovers and consolidation in the industry would not adversely affect the welfare of travelers.

In the 1980s Andrew Carron and Robert Litan studied an industry in which deregulation, in part, brought about one of the sorriest and costliest problems that would have to be faced in the 1990s. Carron wrote three Brookings books about the emerging crisis in the financial sector. His 1982 study of the plight of the thrift industry has proved to be one of the most important studies of financial services to emerge in recent decades. Unfortunately, his message about the impending crisis did not immediately resonate in wider circles. Carron, using a computer model to forecast the financial health of most of the nation's savings and loan institutions, found more than a quarter of them in dubious shape in 1982 and unlikely to survive as independent organizations. He argued for new resources and greater flexibility for the Federal Savings and Loan Insurance Corporation, sought a long-range policy for deregulating interest rates payable on deposits, and proposed means for regulators to identify troubled institutions early on so that they could intervene with merger or subsidy plans.

Since Carron's departure Robert Litan has continued to study banking and the consequences of the restructuring of the financial industry. He traced both the historic pattern of regulation and the changing nature of the market for financial services that had brought banks into competition with the insurance, securities, and real estate industries. He advocated an approach to deregulation that would separate the deposit-taking from the lending activities of all financial conglomerates.

In 1985 the group of economists who had been studying discrete sectors of the economy—primarily Crandall, Litan, and Winston—began to look for some broad organizing themes that might link their policy concerns as well as highlight the microeconomic work under way in an institution long noted for its macroeconomic studies. Their efforts were also intended to elicit financial support from new sources. Two years later Brookings established a new Center for Economic Progress and Employment within its Economic Studies program.

The center, evolving out of staff research interests, took shape in conversations with Ford Foundation staff members and, more important, members of the Brookings board. Indeed, Robert Litan describes Donald Perkins, the retired chairman of Jewel Companies and a member of both the Brookings and Ford Foundation boards, as the "key mover" behind the center. "He pushed me," acknowledges Litan. "He cared about jobs and education and constantly asked the question: what are American workers going to do? He helped think up projects. Even the center's title was Perkins's idea." Perkins was also instrumental in raising funds for the new center, including grants totaling $2 million from the Ford Foundation and a cluster of six-figure corporate gifts.

The center set out to address two major challenges facing the United States—how to improve American living standards and how to create increasing numbers of well-paying jobs. The economists envisioned a research program that would build on Brookings interests in productivity growth and the body of empirical work on specific industries. They would also address questions such as the performance of workers in the workplace, the distribution of earnings, regional changes in the location of American industry, and the commercialization of technological innovation. Perkins and his colleagues, who had often pressed for more "real world research," in Litan's phrase, saw the center as a place capable of studying glaring national problems and setting out some remedies.

The center's first crop of books in the late 1980s examined the threats and challenges to American living standards, speculated on how a future of lousy, low-paying jobs for American workers could be averted, and asked how rates of productivity growth could be increased and paid for. Duplicating earlier formulas for the institution's most successful projects, the center drew upon a sizable cadre of university-based scholars. In 1988 it also introduced a new journal, a microeconomics issue of the *Brookings Papers on Economic Activity,* which has been critical in linking the center's work to that of university economists.

The forces that typically shape Brookings research projects are an inchoate mix of a scholar's practical concern about emerging issues, a sense that policies have not worked as well as they might, a feeling that there are research gaps to be filled, an urge to link discipline-driven theoretical questions to policy applications, and the hard fiscal realities of raising research funds. Over time, the broader research agendas at

Brookings evolve out of the interplay between the staff members' interests and disciplinary research tools and the shifting inventory of problems facing the nation.

Where books are the order of the day and where senior scholars have invested their careers in developing expertise in specific areas, the evolution of a research program is necessarily gradual. A specialized research staff cannot immediately and successfully bend its interests to address newly perceived problems, nor should it necessarily try to do so. There may be other institutions more adequately prepared for research on an emerging issue. And as staff members at Brookings will sometimes confess, not every problem is researchable; the toolbox of the social scientist and policy analyst does not necessarily hold equipment for every policy task.

In the 1990s Brookings economists will retain on their agenda the enduring problems of productivity growth, America's role in the world economy, and the structure of jobs. They look toward the prospects of expanding and reviving older interests in social policy, building upon their work on health care and medical costs. As they look toward a new decade, they also move tentatively toward new fields, contemplating whether their tools are capable of yielding practical answers to questions about the restructuring of socialist economies or of shedding light on worldwide environmental problems.

New World Views

The late 1970s and early 1980s were years of heightened international tension during which the United States embarked on a period of extraordinary increases in military spending. The intellectual framework was familiar since it was still largely shaped by questions posed since the end of World War II about how best to contain and deter an expansive Soviet Union. But broad intellectual frameworks for policy research and discussion do not remain forever fixed. The epoch-shattering international events of 1989 toppled not only the barriers between East and West but the intellectual girders of American foreign policy thinking as well.

The dynamics propelling the changes were already well at work and discernible to some. As John Steinbruner observed in mid-1990, "Much of it seems obvious in retrospect."[4] But experts were nonetheless humbled in 1989, failing to anticipate both the pace and the timing of events. Steinbruner, who taught at Harvard and Yale before taking over as director of the Foreign Policy Studies program in 1978, has shaped the Brookings research agenda on international affairs in very different policy eras; the old era was still defined by postwar orthodoxies, the new will be shaped by principles and ideas only now taking shape.

In the late 1970s, with the United States embarking on modernization of its nuclear forces and improvements in its conventional force structure, Steinbruner thought the Foreign Policy Studies program had several tasks—clarifying technical arguments, serving as an "external whistleblower" in assessing the analyses of others, and working toward conceptual innovations that might reorient discussion of foreign policy. The first task was especially important as the rapid Reagan defense buildup hit a fiscal wall in mid-decade. Claiming that technical arguments among the mandarins of national security were often "abstruse and subject to bias," he and such mainstays of the defense program as William Kaufmann, Martin Binkin, Michael MccGwire, Bruce Blair, Thomas McNaugher, Paul Stares, Richard Betts, and Joshua Epstein aimed to translate the experts' arguments into terms comprehensible to journalists, political leaders, and the public. Like their colleagues in economics, who sought to demystify the policy implications of the president's budget, they worked to reveal the strategic choices implicit in the defense budget.

In a series called Studies in Defense Policy, the Brookings defense analysts looked at particular weapons systems, as in Richard Betts's two volumes on cruise missiles. They devoted much attention to conventional forces in studies such as William Kaufmann's retrospective on *Planning Conventional Forces, 1950–80* (1982). While the administration pushed eagerly toward a 600-ship navy, Kaufmann and MccGwire looked at the uses of naval forces. And with mounting complaints about fraud and abuse at the Pentagon, Thomas McNaugher looked at the perennial issue of reforming military procurement. Martin Binkin and various collaborators continued to address a host of military manpower issues, examining the all-volunteer force, pay and compensation levels, the status of blacks in the military, and the demands that complex military technologies placed on the skills of servicemen and women.

Beginning in 1985, with volumes in the series written by William Kaufmann, Joshua Epstein, and Lawrence Korb, Brookings held the annual defense budget up to scrutiny. In volume after volume, Brookings analysts sought to link spending plans more carefully to sound strategic objectives. They were often critical of aspects of the Reagan defense buildup. They faulted its rapid pace, finding overspending on research, development, and procurement at the cost of operational budgets. And they proposed ways in which military resources could be allocated more efficiently. More fundamentally, they found flaws in the Pentagon planning process stretching back over several decades. Exaggerations of the Soviet threat, neglect of intelligence-gathering and rigorous intelligence assessment, the long-standing competition among the military services, and loose management from above had all contributed to poor management of the resources devoted to national defense.

In addition to its focus on immediate policy choices, the foreign policy research staff sought to contribute to the experts' discussion. A considerable segment of the audience for Brookings research is composed of people already engaged in national security debates. Steinbruner and his colleagues knew that the experts' debate inevitably precedes the public dialogue on issues. Steinbruner explained that "innovative ideas and policy conceptions usually must gain some currency in the world of the experts before they have any systematic, sustained effect on policy decisions."[5]

Since the 1940s and 1950s the tools and concepts for analyzing defense and national security issues had been grounded in game theory and deterrence theory. Over the years, intellectual innovation had simply rung changes on those theories through such concepts as strategic vulnerability, flexible response, and competitive risk taking. Although discrete issues may change with new technological developments, innovative theoretical insight comes relatively slowly to fields that are problem driven and fixated on immediate policy issues or driven by technological advance, as defense analysis so often is. Moreover, the analysis of nuclear war and its prevention has generally proceeded on fundamentally ahistorical assumptions, which early on severed thinking about nuclear strategy from the human experience of warfare.

In the 1980s the Brookings research program worked along two lines of inquiry that pushed strategic studies forward onto new conceptual ground. Steinbruner and colleagues such as Bruce Blair and Richard Betts explored the command and control of strategic forces. They looked at the decisionmaking process that might lead to the use of nuclear weapons. They looked at the actual operating circumstances in the organizations that commanded the weapons. Bruce Blair's *Strategic Command and Control: Redefining the Nuclear Threat* (1985) pointed to the neglect of the nuclear command, control, communications, and intelligence systems, arguing that their deficiencies, both organizational and technological, cast doubt on the U.S. deterrence strategy as well as on the capacity for flexible response. The tendency of strategists and policymakers to be obsessed with the size and survivability of nuclear arsenals rather than command and control structures has led to comforting but misleading judgments about the U.S. ability to retaliate against a nuclear attack and to do so with appropriate deliberation. Blair concluded that a doctrine of "no immediate second use" would promote stability and foster deployment of better command, control, and intelligence networks.

Richard Betts's work, *Surprise Attack: Lessons for Defense Planning* (1982) and *Nuclear Blackmail and Nuclear Balance* (1987), added a historical and a psychological dimension to strategic analysis. Analyzing the historic success of surprise attacks since World War II, Betts argued that it was not primarily intelligence failures that were at fault but the perceptual failures and miscalculations of leaders. Surprise attacks so quickly alter military equations that Betts urged defense planners and policymakers to adopt measures to reduce their vulnerability to surprise and to structure their forces so that surprise attacks could be more readily absorbed and answered. He argued that communications and intelligence systems and the coordination of allied decisionmaking must be improved; greater resources must be devoted to combat readiness and mobility; and arms control and verification agreements must gain higher priority.

Broad concepts are not unrelated to the development of rigorous analytic tools, and the work of Joshua Epstein pressed forward with new models. Epstein, who prepared two volumes in the defense budget series and wrote a book on strategy and force planning in the Persian Gulf, also completed two theoretical books, *The Calculus of Conventional War: Dynamic Analysis without Lanchester Theory* (1985) and *Conventional Force Reductions: A Dynamic Analysis* (1990). Challenging the "bean counting" analysts whose defense assessments are based on static numbers that count troops, tanks, and artillery pieces and weigh them against one another, Epstein argued that quantitative analyses of military forces typically neglect qualitative and operational differences that become all too apparent when military units pursue particular missions. Analyses of military forces are intrinsically flawed when they remain static accountings of inventory. Epstein built mathematical models that incorporate factors such as speed of deployment, tactical choices, qualitative advantages in weaponry, and logistical support. His reassessment of the balance of conventional forces offered a critical tool for judging the Reagan defense program and for elevating debates on national security in an era of cutbacks.

Whether focusing on defense or diplomacy, relations between the Soviet Union and United States were central to the Brookings Foreign Policy program throughout the 1980s. In 1981 Stephen Kaplan and his colleagues produced a volume, *Diplomacy of Power: Soviet Armed Force as a Political Instrument*, on the Soviet Union's use of force since 1945. By the end of the decade Michael MccGwire had completed a study of changing Soviet military doctrine and national security. In 1980 Jerry Hough completed *Soviet Leadership in Transition*, the first of a cluster of studies on the inner workings of the Soviet Union. Those studies have included Ed A. Hewett's books, *Energy, Economics, and Foreign Policy in the Soviet Union* (1984) and *Reforming the Soviet Economy: Equality vs. Efficiency* (1988), and Hough's *Opening Up the Soviet Economy* (1988), which have related the saga of falling growth rates, macroeconomic and microeconomic imbalances, waste, and low rates of technological change in the Soviet Union. Indeed, the analysis of the Soviet economic plight and the hard policy choices facing Soviet leaders provided early insights into the crisis that would beset Gorbachev in the late 1980s. Hewett's work, in particular, has provided a framework for assessing past Soviet economic performance and understanding the difficulties facing reformers. His 1988 study, overtly linked in its title to Arthur Okun's work, sets out the trade-offs facing a society in which markets must be created anew. Without predicting success or failure in the restructuring of the Soviet economy, Hewett's counsel to U.S. policymakers is one of cautious watchfulness.

Diplomatic relations between the United States and the Soviet Union were the subject of much of Raymond Garthoff's work. Garthoff, who spent thirty years in the State Department, including participation in the ABM and SALT I negotiations and service as ambassador to Bulgaria, witnessed the gaps in perception between the two adversaries. His historically grounded studies of the Cuban missile crisis, intelligence assessment, and the strategic balance culminated in his voluminous *Détente and Confrontation: American-Soviet Relations from Nixon to Reagan* (1985). It traced the development and then disintegration of the two nation's relations between 1969 and 1984.

Problems with the policy of détente were present from the outset, Garthoff argued, as he took the architects of the policy to task. The goals of détente were never clearly articulated or agreed on. Bringing both the practitioner's insights and the detachment of the diplomatic historian to his analysis, Garthoff's work focused on the adversaries' perceptions of each other and how their respective political systems reinforced those perceptions. He concluded that both superpowers shared responsibility for the demise of détente.

Brookings continued its work in specific regions of the world. Harry Harding left Stanford University to take up Barnett's mantle as the institution's China scholar and build on his studies of Chinese politics. In *China's Second Revolution: Reform after Mao* (1987) Harding chronicled the demise of Maoist revolutionary dreams and charted the political and economic advances in the decade after Mao's death. He foresaw the spasms as China lurched between reform and retrenchment, with economic reform proceeding at a more rapid pace than political liberalization.

After joining Brookings in 1984, Edward J. Lincoln continued the institution's line of work on the Japanese economy with two books, *Japan: Facing Economic Maturity* (1988) and *Japan's Unequal Trade* (1990). With the postwar Japanese economic "miracle" at an end by the early 1970s, Lincoln provided an overview of the Japanese economy from 1973 to 1987, paying special attention to financial deregulation. Seeing Japan as a mature economy, he asked how Japan could best respond to the imbalance between high levels of personal savings and low corporate demands for investment. In his second book he examined Japan's "peculiar trading pattern" and the reasons that Western nations have found access to its maturity so difficult. He argued that a century-long effort to catch up with the West had left a legacy of interlocking institutions, behavioral patterns, and attitudes that gave Western nations no choice but to exert continuing pressure on Japan to open its markets.

Work on the Middle East took on new urgency after the fall of the shah of Iran. During the 1980s William Quandt wrote and edited volumes on the Camp David accords and the peace process in the Middle East, drawing on his insights as a member of the U.S. delegation at Camp David. He also completed two books on Saudi Arabia. Quandt's arrival at Brookings and the willingness of the defense analysts, especially McNaugher and Epstein, to look at the Persian Gulf transformed Brookings into a leading center of study of the Middle East. As the decade ended, Brookings was beginning to rebuild competence in Latin American studies and looking for the first time at Africa.

The Brookings Foreign Policy Studies program had been molded by assumptions that did not have to be discarded as the dramatic events of 1989 unfolded. Brookings had tracked more closely than most other research institutions the changing economic circumstances in the Soviet Union and had analyzed changing Soviet security policy and the dissolution of its military alliance. It was also in the forefront as events unfolded in the Persian Gulf. Nonetheless, Brookings researchers were quick to concede that there were limits to what they knew. They believed that new assumptions had to be set out to guide the research program in the 1990s. Tentatively, John Steinbruner laid out the implications of what was clearly a revolution in foreign policy. He sought to discern "the inherent logic to the emerging era" and "the apparent mandate of events."

The imperatives of the new era, Steinbruner suggested, could be found in the concepts of cooperative security and economic engagement.[6] The former meant that both the United States and the Soviet Union had to begin to acknowledge a shared interest in reducing the costs of national security and that both had to rethink how security arrangements would be organized as traditional alliance systems broke down. At the same time, the notion of economic engagement would set in motion a search for mechanisms to integrate the failed socialist economies of the East with the economies of the capitalist West. As Steinbruner and his colleagues understood, the pace and scope of international events had outstripped the ability of experts and the public alike to comprehend them. In an era of epoch-making changes, routine think tank tasks—analyzing policy proposals, weighing alternatives, building intellectual consensus—were thrust aside by the effort to grasp the underlying meaning of events and to discern what kinds of expertise might be relevant to the new epoch.

CONCLUSION:
TOWARD INTELLIGENT
DEMOCRACY

THE ROLE of a think tank can never be static. In its evolution, Brookings has passed through several phases, with each era leaving its imprint on what the institution has become. As an efficiency bureau in the 1910s and 1920s, Brookings worked on managerial and budgeting procedures for federal and state agencies. It offered a practical graduate curriculum, propelling students toward public service careers and awarding doctoral degrees in the 1920s. It served as an independent, sometimes querulous, voice criticizing government policies and programs in the 1930s and 1940s. It first offered educational programs for federal executives and other professional groups in the late 1950s. It toiled as an adjunct to government research and planning departments, helping policymakers in tasks of planning and evaluation in the 1960s and 1970s. It devised ways of reaching out to the Washington press corps and the broader public in the 1980s. And throughout its history it has sustained one of the nation's most distinguished programs of applied policy research, while publishing approximately 1,500 books.

Applied research—forging practical analytic tools out of social science insights and putting realistic policy choices to the test of analysis—has been at the heart of the institution's work for seventy-five years.

Organizations that survive as long as Brookings has, in the dynamic environment it inhabits, must exhibit considerable powers of adaptability. Although Brookings is a venerable institution on the national political scene, like all policy research institutions it is an inherently dependent and sometimes fragile entity that adapts to—and simultaneously works to reshape—diverse external forces. Situated on the boundaries of several sectors of American society—philanthropy, education, and government—the institution's place can best be comprehended by examining its interaction with those institutions. Its future can be glimpsed only by asking how its relations with those other sectors will evolve.

Brookings was a creature of American private philanthropy and has been dependent through most of its history on the nation's largest foundations, adjusting to changes in foundation policies and priorities while seeking to tap new reservoirs of philanthropic support. By the standards of other policy research institutions, Brookings is enviably well-off. An endowment on the scale of the institution's offers a modicum of security, and a seventy-fifth anniversary campaign to raise $34 million ($11 million for endowment) will ensure a fair margin of continued autonomy for Brookings. But by the standards of research universities, its resources are small and the sources it can draw on for financial support are limited and often oriented toward relatively short-term projects rather than toward long-term social research.

The quest for financial resources is a curious interplay among Brookings scholars, foundation executives, and other prospective supporters. This search for resources is a dialogue in which policy experts and social scientists interact with foundation executives and others who control philanthropic funds. The scholars are equipped with research tools and practical insights into issues, the funders occupy a high vantage point from which to assess emerging problems and judge the work of diverse research institutions, policy advocates and activists, and others who are at work in the political arena. In many respects, the give-and-take between Brookings and potential supporters, although removed from our formal political institutions, marks the beginning of policy deliberation in the United States. The search for funds defines a "politics of knowledge," as one scholar describes it, that shapes research agendas on emerging policy issues, sanctifies particular kinds of professional expertise, and endows some institutions with the prestige and financial resources to make a mark on public policy deliberation.

Brookings is also dependent on the academic community. With only forty to fifty senior scholars in residence, Brookings cannot cover all fields. Nor can a cadre of analysts whose focus tends to be on practical affairs and real-world policy problems expect to push ahead on the frontiers of theory. The scholars can refine some analytic tools, observe and describe events carefully, debate and test practical courses of action, but in the long run their work must rely on the wider university community of social scientists where basic social science scholarship is done and where new generations of researchers receive their training.

Yet even though Brookings is always dependent on developments in the academic world, in many ways it also serves as a countervailing force to the abstruse theorizing and mind-numbing empiricism of the university. It must continually compete for first-rank policy scholars, while holding out to them a career that is more loosely structured, not nearly so strictly ordered by academic discipline and theory, teaching, and intellectual detachment from the events of the day. Rooted in an environment in which it must also interact with policymakers, business executives, and journalists, Brookings researchers put the social sciences to the test in a world where the real and the doable matter. Charles Schultze once said of Kermit Gordon that "he looked for specific and realistic answers to specific and real problems, one by one." The same might be said of the institution. It has always been simultaneously a collaborator and a competitor with university social science departments.

Brookings also operates on the boundaries of government. Its scholars are connected to policymakers and government executives in countless informal ways, from casual conversations and congressional testimony to formal conference programs and, at times during its long history, contract research projects. Inevitably research is mediated and diffused by complex chains—policy advisory staffs, academic and professional networks, and the media. The lines of influence on governmental decisionmaking are so fluid and the flow of ideas so subtle and intricate that they can scarcely be sketched in rough hand, let alone precisely modeled. Lines of cause and effect remain elusive.

The Brookings Institution plays several roles, but one consistent long-term effect is clear. Brookings has been centrally engaged in creating the body of policy experts and analysts that has become so important to policymaking processes in the twentieth century. Brookings scholars, involved in the early stages with the Bureau of the Budget, the Council of Economic Advisers, the Policy Planning Staff, and the Congressional Budget Office, have helped reshape the expert advisory networks in and out of government.

Moreover, when few scholars have been available and prepared to tackle an emerging policy issue, Brookings has often worked to redirect scholarly attention and fashion new networks of expertise, whether on government finance and regulation, the economies of Asian nations, or the command and control of nuclear weapons. Indeed, the single best test of the institution's long-term success and influence resides not in its immediate impact on particular policy decisions—a hit-or-miss matter at best—but on its ability to shape expert networks in ways that continue to anticipate the nation's problems even before the contours of policy debate are delineated.

Those contours are often shaped by policies and events that are already in the process of unfolding. From its early concern with administrative matters to its later work evaluating policy options and assessing the effectiveness of various programs, Brookings scholars have studied how government works and asked what might make it work better. The definitions of efficiency and effectiveness have changed, as have the techniques for studying and measuring them, but the conviction that a reasoned, dispassionate, and scientific approach can make government work better has remained at the heart of the institution's efforts.

The initial, perhaps naive, hope that social science could arbitrate among diverse interests and cool political passions has long since evaporated. If the institution's lengthy experience teaches only one lesson, it is that empirical research and reasoned analysis will never eliminate the uncertainty inherent in policy decisions, nor will it provide authoritative resolution when different values are in conflict. In recent years, it has often seemed that social science is nothing more than a forensic weapon, with social scientists acting as well-armed guns for hire. Their contests seem merely to aggravate a deeply divided government and a profoundly sundered polity.

Recognizing that we are afflicted by a government—and a polity—that is more deeply divided than the founders ever contemplated when they devised a mixed regime of checks and balances, Brookings has often seen its job as one of understanding and bridging those divides by means of research and communication. Yet the disciplined approach to research and the commitment to evaluate the options inevitably temper policy discourse. They ground expectations in reality.

Situated outside our political institutions and the bureaucracy, Brookings can span a fragmented government. In our society, where there is wide latitude for nongovernmental institutions to take part in policymaking, Brookings also helps link those private organizations to the policy process. And since through most of its history it has tried to situate itself at the center of the political spectrum, it is among the institutions that have most routinely shaped an elite consensus on issues. It acts as one of the gravitational forces that pulls our politics back toward pragmatic questions about the realistic and the workable.

For all it has accomplished, however, Brookings can offer something else that is vitally important in our democracy—something that has perhaps been overlooked in the seventy-five years since the founders of the Institute for Government Research first raised the standard of efficient government. It is in part the challenge to which an adaptive institution must respond as it looks at the problems that afflict our government and that create a divide between the governed and the governors.

The generation that set Brookings in motion spoke of "efficient citizenship," a term that now sounds awkward and incongruous. But it implied that the expert's specialized knowledge, and the administrative competence that was its corollary, was not the sole intelligence or competence required in a democracy. Rather, there was a broader democratic intelligence to which the expert had to contribute as well. It was not limited to the expert networks where the creative, administrative, and critical intelligence—the forms of intelligence of which Lyndon Johnson spoke in celebrating the first half century of work at Brookings—comes into play. Over the years the work at Brookings has added admirably to the intellectual capital that political leaders and their advisers have at their command in setting priorities and choosing among policy alternatives. But the wider arena of democratic choice has yet to be so well served by our expert institutions. Surely, the challenge as Brookings looks toward the next century is to ask how it might nurture the democratic intelligence and enlarge the circle of reasoned and informed deliberation.

NOTES

Notes to the Prologue

1. On the early planning for the fiftieth anniversary see Fiftieth Anniversary Committee, 1964–65, Special Observances, box 3, especially the memorandum from Charles B. Saunders to Robert Calkins, "Anniversary Planning," September 23, 1965, Brookings Institution Archives. Brookings staff members suggested the subject matter and volunteered to work with the presidential staff in research and preparation of the president's speech. Johnson's speech and the introductory remarks of Eugene R. Black and Robert Calkins were published in a pamphlet, *Government and the Critical Intelligence: An Address by Lyndon B. Johnson and Remarks by Eugene R. Black and Robert D. Calkins* (Brookings, 1966).

2. Robert Wood, "The Great Society in 1984: Relic or Reality?" in Marshall Kaplan and Peggy Cuciti, eds., *The Great Society and Its Legacy* (Duke University Press, 1986), p. 19.

3. On those subjects see James Allen Smith, *The Idea Brokers: Think Tanks and the Rise of the New Policy Elite* (Free Press, 1991).

4. The story of Johnson's relationship with the intellectual community is related in Eric Goldman's memoir of government service, *The Tragedy of Lyndon Johnson* (Alfred A. Knopf, 1968).

5. Black, "Remarks," in *Government and the Critical Intelligence*, p. 2.

Notes to Chapter One

1. On the history of the Institute for Government Research see Charles Thomson, *The Institute for Government Research* (Brookings, 1956); and Donald T. Critchlow, *The Brookings Institution, 1916–52: Expertise and the Public Interest in a Democratic Society* (Northern Illinois University Press, 1984).

2. On the Taft Commission, the movement for a national budget, and a comparative history of the Bureau of the Budget (now the Office of Management and Budget) and the General Accounting Office, see Frederick C. Mosher, *A Tale of Two Agencies: A Comparative Analysis of the General Accounting Office and the Office of Management and Budget* (Louisiana State University Press, 1984).

3. Institute for Government Research, *Prospectus,* May 1, 1915, Brookings Institution Archives (BIA).

4. Nearly forty years after the founding of the Institute for Government Research, several of the original trustees wrote about the institute's beginnings. "Materials Relating to Published and Unpublished Histories, 1914–66," especially the letter of Jerome D. Greene to Robert Calkins, April 19, 1954, BIA.

5. Institute for Government Research, *Public Prospectus,* March 13, 1916, BIA.

6. Hermann Hagedorn, *Brookings: A Biography* (Macmillan and Company, 1936), p. 261.

7. Harold G. Moulton, "Mr. Brookings and the Institution He Founded," May 22, 1950, Administration, Special Observances, 100th Anniversary of Robert S. Brookings's Birth, box 1, BIA.

8. Institute of Economics, *Prospectus,* 1922, BIA.

9. Institute of Economics, By-laws, BIA.

10. Robert Brookings is quoted in Charles B. Saunders, Jr., *The Brookings Institution: A Fifty-Year History* (Brookings, 1966), p. 36.

11. Saunders, *Brookings Institution,* p. 37.

12. Robert Brookings Graduate School, "Report of Walton Hamilton to the Board of Trustees of the Brookings School," April 30, 1926, BIA.

13. Robert Brookings Graduate School, "First Plan Presented by Drafting Committee," BIA.

Notes to Chapter Two

1. Hugh Johnson, United Features syndicated columns, April 23, 1934, and April 24, 1935.

2. Stuart Chase, "Saving and Spending," *Survey Graphic* (November 1935), p. 533.

3. This quotation is from the newsletter, *UAW-CIO Ammunition,* September 1949, cited in "Reviews and Comments on Brookings Publications," Publications Programs, BIA.

4. "Brookings Pop Gun," *Nation*, October 21, 1944, p. 452.

5. The volumes were *America's Capacity to Produce* (1933); *America's Capacity to Consume* (1934); *The Formation of Capital* (1935); and *Income and Economic Progress* (1935).

6. On the approach to the depression recommended by Moulton and his colleagues see Harold G. Moulton and others, *Income and Economic Progress* (Brookings, 1935), pp. 24–27.

7. Chase, "Saving and Spending," p. 536.

8. Harold G. Moulton, *The New Philosophy of Public Debt* (Brookings, 1943), p. 88.

9. Harold G. Moulton, *Controlling Factors in Economic Development* (Brookings, 1949), p. 148.

10. Joseph H. Willits, "Memorandum concerning Jerome Greene," May 9, 1947, Record Group 2 (General Correspondence), box 366, folder 2479–200, Brookings Institution, Rockefeller Foundation, Rockefeller Archive Center, Pocantico Hills, New York.

Notes to Chapter Three

1. Charles B. Saunders, Jr., *The Brookings Institution: A Fifty-Year History*, p. 82.

2. Docket Excerpt, Executive Committee of Board of Trustees, September 25, 1958, Grant 58-390, Ford Foundation Archives, New York.

3. "The Private Research Organization," interview with Robert Calkins, *Challenge: Magazine of Economic Affairs*, vol. 12 (February 1964), pp. 18–21.

Notes to Chapter Four

1. Edited transcript of an interview with Steven Roberts, July 28, 1965, President's General Files—Kermit Gordon, BIA.

2. Kermit Gordon is quoted in "Powerhouse of Economic Thought," *Business Week*, June 5, 1965, pp. 124–29.

3. Gordon volunteered the observation in an interview with the St. Louis *Post-Dispatch*, July 10, 1967.

4. Kermit A. Gordon, "How Much Should Government Do?" *Saturday Review*, January 9, 1965, pp. 25–27, 76.

5. Gordon is quoted in *National Journal*, February 12, 1972, p. 253.

6. Kermit Gordon, ed., *Agenda for the Nation* (Brookings, 1968), p. 3.

7. Gordon, *Agenda for the Nation*, p. 5.

8. Edwin Dale, *New York Times Book Review*, January 26, 1969.

9. Kermit Gordon, "The President's Review," *Brookings Annual Report, 1970*, pp. 1–2.

10. Gilbert Steiner to Kermit Gordon, "Review of Program, Performance, and Priorities," May 27, 1975, BIA.

11. On the project see Richard Nathan, *Social Science in Government: Uses and Misuses* (Basic Books, 1988), pp. 151–73.

12. Nathan, *Social Science in Government*, pp. 174–87.

13. Brookings Institution, 1971–74, Memorandum, "Services to Congress Provided by Brookings Staff Members," September 5, 1973, Rockefeller Brothers Fund Files, Rockefeller Archive Center, Pocantico Hills, New York.

14. Kermit Gordon, "The President's Review," *Biennial Report, 1968–69* (Brookings, 1970), pp. 1–2.

Notes to Chapter Five

1. Kermit Gordon quoted in the *Brookings Bulletin*, vol. 13 (Fall–Winter 1976), p. 3.

2. Arthur M. Okun, National Public Radio interview, transcript in the *Brookings Bulletin*, vol. 12 (Summer 1975).

3. Arthur Okun, *Equality and Efficiency: The Big Tradeoff* (Brookings, 1975), p. 120.

4. Craufurd D. Goodwin, ed., *Exhortation and Controls: The Search for a Wage-Price Policy, 1945–71* (Brookings, 1975); Arnold R. Weber, *In Pursuit of Price Stability: The Wage-Price Freeze of 1971* (Brookings, 1973); Robert F. Lanzillotti, Mary T. Hamilton, and R. Blaine Roberts, *Phase II in Review: The Price Commission Experience* (Brookings, 1975); and Arnold R. Weber and Daniel J. B. Mitchell, *The Pay Board's Progress: Wage Controls in Phase II* (Brookings, 1978).

5. Charles L. Schultze, with Edward K. Hamilton and Allen Schick, *Setting National Priorities: The 1971 Budget* (Brookings, 1970), p. 4.

Notes to Chapter Six

1. The various phrases characterizing Brookings have been culled from newspaper and news magazine articles about the institution that have appeared over the past thirty years; the words describing Brookings books are drawn from a sampling of book reviews over the same period.

2. The memo from Haldeman to Cole, May 1, 1969, is published in Bruce Oudes, ed., *From: The President—Richard Nixon's Secret Files* (Harper and Row, 1989), p. 29.

3. Richard Nixon, *RN: The Memoirs of Richard Nixon* (Grosset and Dunlap, 1978), p. 512.

4. Memo from T. C. Huston to H. R. Haldeman, July 16, 1970, in Oudes, *From: The President*, pp. 147–48. Another inside account of the plans to firebomb Brookings is in John Ehrlichman, *Witness to Power: The Nixon Years* (Simon and Schuster, 1982), p. 403.

5. Memo from T. C. Huston to H. R. Haldeman, July 16, 1970, in Oudes, *From: The President*, pp. 147–48.

6. Memo from Patrick Buchanan to Richard Nixon, November 10, 1972, in Oudes, *From: The President*, p. 564.

7. Letter from Kermit Gordon to Peter Flanigan, October 20, 1971, Personal Papers of Kermit Gordon, box 22, BIA.

8. He spoke to a reporter for an article in the *National Journal*, February 12, 1972, p. 257.

9. Quoted in the *National Journal*, February 12, 1972.

10. Board of Trustees minutes, May 1972, BIA.

11. Board of Trustees minutes, October 1973, BIA.

12. Memorandum from Henry Owen to Kermit Gordon, undated (probably April 1969), President's General Files—Kermit Gordon, 1968–69, BIA.

13. Memorandum from Robert Asher to Henry Owen, April 14, 1969, President's General Files—Kermit Gordon, 1968–69, BIA.

Notes to Chapter Seven

1. A. Doak Barnett, quoted in the *Brookings Bulletin*, vol. 13 (Fall–Winter 1976), p. 4.

2. James MacGregor Burns, quoted in the *Brookings Bulletin*, vol. 13 (Fall–Winter 1976), p. 4.

3. Appendix C contains financial summaries.

4. The phrase "ideas industry" was used by Richard Reeves, *The Reagan Detour* (Simon and Schuster, 1985).

5. Plans were presented and approved at the spring meeting of the Board of Trustees, 1981, BIA.

6. Gilbert Steiner is quoted in Martin Tolchin, "Brookings Thinks about Its Future," *New York Times*, December 14, 1983.

7. Quoted in Tolchin, "Brookings Thinks about Its Future."

8. Robert Calkins in the foreword to Douglass Cater, *Developing Leadership in Government: An Account of the Brookings Conferences for Federal Executives, 1957–59* (Brookings, 1960), pp. 2, 17.

9. Cater, *Developing Leadership*, p. 6.

10. On the status of the program in the mid-1970s see Walter Held's report in the *Brookings Bulletin*, vol. 13 (Fall–Winter 1976), pp. 16–19, and also Richard Simons to Walter Held, "1975 Review of Program, Performance, and Priorities," September 3, 1975, BIA.

11. On the early years of the program see Mark W. Cannon and Warren I. Cikins, "Interbranch Cooperation in Improving the Administration of Justice: A Major Innovation," *Washington and Lee Law Review*, vol. 38 (Winter 1981), pp. 1–20.

12. Board of Trustees minutes, May 1980, BIA.

13. Board of Trustees minutes, June 1983, BIA.

Notes to Chapter Eight

1. Martha Derthick, Board of Trustees minutes, May 1979, BIA.
2. A. James Reichley, *Conservatives in an Age of Change: The Nixon and Ford Administrations* (Brookings, 1981), pp. 418–19.
3. Martha Derthick, Board of Trustees minutes, May 1979, BIA.
4. Thomas E. Mann, Board of Trustees minutes, May 1990, BIA.

Notes to Chapter Nine

1. Alice Rivlin, Board of Trustees minutes, June 1983, BIA.
2. See, for example, Robert Kuttner, "Tax Reform: Where Credit Is Due," *Business Week,* June 2, 1986.
3. Lester Lave, *The Strategy of Social Regulation* (Brookings, 1981), p. 4.
4. John Steinbruner, Board of Trustees minutes, May 1990, BIA.
5. John Steinbruner, Board of Trustees minutes, May 1979, BIA.
6. John D. Steinbruner, "Revolution in Foreign Policy," in Henry J. Aaron, ed., *Setting National Priorities: Policy for the Nineties* (Brookings, 1990), pp. 65–109.

APPENDIX A:
A BROOKINGS
BIBLIOGRAPHY, 1966–90

1966

Economic Studies

Barlow, Robin, and others. *Economic Behavior of the Affluent.*
Bolton, Roger E. *Defense Purchases and Regional Growth.*
Brittain, John A. *Corporate Dividend Policy.*
Brown, Robert T. *Transport and the Economic Integration of South America.*
Colm, Gerhard, and Peter Wagner. *Federal Budget Projections.*
Comiez, Maynard S. *A Capital Budget Statement for the U.S. Government.*
Keith, E. Gordon, ed. *Foreign Tax Policies and Economic Growth.* A Report of
  the National Bureau of Economic Research and the Brookings Institution.
Netzer, Dick. *Economics of the Property Tax.*
Owen, Wilfred. *The Metropolitan Transportation Problem,* rev. ed.
Pechman, Joseph A. *Federal Tax Policy.*
Shoup, Carl S. *Federal Estate and Gift Taxes.*
Wilson, George W., and others. *The Impact of Highway Investment on
  Development.*

Foreign Policy Studies

Frankel, Charles. *The Neglected Aspect of Foreign Affairs: American Educational and Cultural Policy Abroad.*
Sapin, Burton M. *The Making of United States Foreign Policy.*
Westwood, Andrew F. *Foreign Aid in a Foreign Policy Framework.*

Governmental Studies

Cummings, Milton C., ed. *The National Election of 1964.*
Lawrence, Samuel A. *United States Merchant Shipping Policies and Politics.*

Also Published by Brookings

Saunders, Charles B., Jr. *The Brookings Institution: A Fifty-Year History.*

1967

Economic Studies

Break, George F. *Intergovernmental Fiscal Relations in the United States.*
Denison, Edward F. *Why Growth Rates Differ: Postwar Experience in Nine Western Countries.*
Eckstein, Otto, ed. *Studies in the Economics of Income Maintenance.*
Fein, Rashi. *The Doctor Shortage: An Economic Diagnosis.*
Green, Christopher. *Negative Taxes and the Poverty Problem.*
Jantscher, Gerald R. *Trusts and Estate Taxation.*
Nelson, Richard R., Merton J. Peck, and Edward D. Kalachek. *Technology, Economic Growth, and Public Policy.*
Robinson, Marshall A., Herbert C. Morton, and James D. Calderwood. *An Introduction to Economic Reasoning,* 4th ed.
Rothenberg, Jerome. *Economic Evaluation of Urban Renewal.*
Sheahan, John. *The Wage-Price Guideposts.*
Somers, Herman M., and Anne R. Somers. *Medicare and the Hospitals: Issues and Prospects.*

Foreign Policy Studies

Burr, Robert N. *Our Troubled Hemisphere: Perspectives on United States–Latin American Relations.*
Cox, Arthur M. *Prospects for Peacekeeping.*
Hirschman, Albert O. *Development Projects Observed.*
Johnson, Harry G. *Economic Policies toward Less Developed Countries.*
Plank, John, ed. *Cuba and the United States: Long-Range Perspectives.*
Rustow, Dankwart A. *A World of Nations: Problems of Political Modernization.*

Governmental Studies

Jones, Charles O. *Every Second Year: Congressional Behavior and the Two-Year Term.*
Orlans, Harold. *Contracting for Atoms.*
Ripley, Randall B. *Party Leaders in the House of Representatives.*
Stanley, David T., and others. *Men Who Govern: A Biographical Profile of Federal Political Executives.*

1968

Economic Studies

Ando, Albert, E. Cary Brown, and Ann F. Friedlaender, eds. *Studies in Economic Stabilization.*
Caves, Richard E., and others. *Britain's Economic Prospects.*
Chase, Samuel B., Jr., ed. *Problems in Public Expenditure Analysis.*
David, Martin. *Alternative Approaches to Capital Gains Taxation.*
Fromm, Gary, and Paul Taubman. *Policy Simulations with an Econometric Model.*
Hunter, Holland. *Soviet Transport Experience: Its Lessons for Other Countries.*
Katona, George, and Eva Mueller. *Consumer Response to Income Increases: An Investigation Conducted in the Year of the Tax Cut.*
Krause, Lawrence B. *European Economic Integration and the United States.*
Lewis, Wilfred, Jr., ed. *Budget Concepts for Economic Analysis.*
Owen, Wilfred. *Distance and Development: Transport and Communications in India.*

Pechman, Joseph A., Henry J. Aaron, and Michael K. Taussig. *Social Security: Perspectives for Reform.*
Ribich, Thomas I. *Education and Poverty.*

Foreign Policy Studies

Haviland, H. Field, Jr., and others. *Vietnam after the War: Peacekeeping and Rehabilitation.*
Russell, Ruth B. *The United Nations and United States Security Policy.*

Governmental Studies

Danhof, Clarence H. *Government Contracting and Technological Change.*
Gordon, Kermit, ed. *Agenda for the Nation.*
Orlans, Harold, ed. *Science Policy and the University.*
Sundquist, James L. *Politics and Policy: The Eisenhower, Kennedy, and Johnson Years.*

1969

Economic Studies

Friedlaender, Ann F. *The Dilemma of Freight Transport Regulation.*
Haefele, Edwin T., ed. *Transport and National Goals.*
Harberger, Arnold C., and Martin J. Bailey, eds. *The Taxation of Income from Capital.*
Maxwell, James A. *Financing State and Local Governments,* 2d ed.
Netzer, Dick. *State-Local Finance and Intergovernmental Fiscal Relations.*
Ott, David J., and Attiat F. Ott. *Federal Budget Policy,* rev. ed.
Schultze, Charles L. *The Politics and Economics of Public Spending.*
Straszheim, Mahlon R. *The International Airline Industry.*
Thurow, Lester C. *Poverty and Discrimination.*

Governmental Studies

Cleaveland, Frederic N., and associates. *Congress and Urban Problems: A Casebook on the Legislative Process.*

Schmeckebier, Laurence F., and Roy B. Eastin. *Government Publications and Their Use*, 2d ed.

Sundquist, James L. *Making Federalism Work: A Study of Program Coordination at the Community Level.*

1970

Economic Studies

Kershaw, Joseph A. *Government Against Poverty.*

Levin, Henry M., ed. *Community Control of Schools.*

Okun, Arthur M. *The Political Economy of Prosperity.*

Schultze, Charles L. *Setting National Priorities: The 1971 Budget.*

Steiner, Peter O. *Public Expenditure Budgeting.*

Foreign Policy Studies

Asher, Robert E. *Development Assistance in the Seventies: Alternatives for the United States.*

Baldwin, Robert E. *Nontariff Distortions of International Trade.*

Lefever, Ernest W. *Spear and Scepter: Army, Police, and Politics in Tropical Africa.*

Preeg, Ernest H. *Traders and Diplomats: An Analysis of the Kennedy Round of Negotiations under the General Agreement on Tariffs and Trade.*

Governmental Studies

Horn, Stephen. *Unused Power: The Work of the Senate Committee on Appropriations.*

Saunders, Charles B., Jr. *Upgrading the American Police: Education and Training for Better Law Enforcement.*

Sayre, Wallace S., and Judith H. Parris. *Voting for President: The Electoral College and the American Political System.*

1971

Economic Studies

Bach, G. L. *Making Monetary and Fiscal Policy.*
Capron, William M., ed. *Technological Change in Regulated Industries.*
Fromm, Gary, ed. *Tax Incentives and Capital Spending.*
Krause, Lawrence B. *Sequel to Bretton Woods: A Proposal to Reform the World Monetary System.*
Kresge, David T., and Paul O. Roberts. *Systems Analysis and Simulation Models.*
Meyer, John R., and Mahlon R. Straszheim. *Pricing and Project Evaluation.*
Noll, Roger G. *Reforming Regulation: An Evaluation of the Ash Council Proposals.*
Pechman, Joseph A. *Federal Tax Policy,* 2d ed.
Rivlin, Alice M. *Systematic Thinking for Social Action.*
Schultze, Charles L. *The Distribution of Farm Subsidies: Who Gets the Benefits?*
Schultze, Charles L., Edward R. Fried, Alice M. Rivlin, and Nancy H. Teeters. *Setting National Priorities: The 1972 Budget.*
Sorkin, Alan L. *American Indians and Federal Aid.*
Tilton, John E. *International Diffusion of Technology: The Case of Semiconductors.*
Warford, Jeremy J. *Public Policy toward General Aviation.*

Foreign Policy Studies

Barnett, A. Doak. *A New U.S. Policy toward China.*
Fabian, Larry L. *Soldiers without Enemies: Preparing the United Nations for Peacekeeping.*
Kuzmack, Arnold M. *Naval Force Levels and Modernization: An Analysis of Shipbuilding Requirements.*
Newhouse, John. *U.S. Troops in Europe: Issues, Costs, and Choices.*

Governmental Studies

Schick, Allen. *Budget Innovation in the States.*
Stanley, David T., and Marjorie Girth. *Bankruptcy: Problem, Process, Reform.*
Steiner, Gilbert Y. *The State of Welfare.*

1972

Economic Studies

Aaron, Henry J. *Shelter and Subsidies: Who Benefits from Federal Housing Policies?*
Brittain, John A. *The Payroll Tax for Social Security.*
Eads, George C. *The Local Service Airline Experiment.*
Owen, Wilfred. *The Accessible City.*
Schultze, Charles L., Edward R. Fried, Alice M. Rivlin, and Nancy H. Teeters. *Setting National Priorities: The 1973 Budget.*
Wellington, Harry H., and Ralph K. Winter, Jr. *The Unions and the Cities.*

Foreign Policy Studies

Binkin, Martin. *Support Costs in the Defense Budget: The Submerged One-Third.*
Carnoy, Martin. *Industrialization in a Latin American Common Market.*
Grunwald, Joseph, Miguel S. Wionczek, and Martin Carnoy. *Latin American Economic Integration and U.S. Policy.*
Poats, Rutherford M. *Technology for Developing Nations: New Directions for U.S. Technical Assistance.*

Governmental Studies

Dunn, Delmer D. *Financing Presidential Campaigns.*
Goodwin, Leonard. *Do The Poor Want to Work? A Social-Psychological Study of Work Orientations.*
Parris, Judith H. *The Convention Problem: Issues in Reform of Presidential Nominating Procedures.*
Stanley, David T. *Managing Local Government under Union Pressure.*

1973

Economic Studies

Aaron, Henry J. *Why Is Welfare So Hard to Reform?*
Cairncross, Sir Alec. *Control of Long-Term International Capital Movements.*

Fried, Edward R., Alice M. Rivlin, Charles L. Schultze, and Nancy H. Teeters. *Setting National Priorities: The 1974 Budget.*
Krause, Lawrence B., and Walter S. Salant, eds. *European Monetary Unification and Its Meaning for the United States.*
McKinnon, Ronald L. *Money and Capital in Economic Development.*
Noll, Roger G., Merton J. Peck, and John J. McGowan. *Economic Aspects of Television Regulation.*
Reischauer, Robert D., and Robert W. Hartman. *Reforming School Finance.*
Stieber, Jack. *Public Employee Unionism: Structure, Growth, Policy.*
Weber, Arnold R. *In Pursuit of Price Stability: The Wage-Price Freeze of 1971.*

Foreign Policy Studies

Berg, Alan. *The Nutrition Factor: Its Role in National Development.*
Blechman, Barry M. *The Changing Soviet Navy.*
Mason, Edward S., and Robert E. Asher. *The World Bank since Bretton Woods.*
Owen, Henry, ed. *The Next Phase in Foreign Policy.*
Quanbeck, Alton H., and Barry M. Blechman. *Strategic Forces: Issues for the Mid-Seventies.*

Governmental Studies

Bain, Richard C., and Judith H. Parris. *Convention Decisions and Voting Records,* 2d ed.
Kaufman, Herbert. *Administrative Feedback: Monitoring Subordinates' Behavior.*
Matthews, Donald R., ed. *Perspectives on Presidential Selection.*
Sundquist, James L. *Dynamics of the Party System: Alignment and Realignment of Political Parties in the United States.*

1974

Economic Studies

Blechman, Barry M., Edward M. Gramlich, and Robert W. Hartman. *Setting National Priorities: The 1975 Budget.*
Blinder, Alan S., and others. *The Economics of Public Finance.*

Breyer, Stephen G., and Paul W. MacAvoy. *Energy Regulation by the Federal Power Commission.*
Denison, Edward F. *Accounting for United States Economic Growth, 1929–1969.*
Douglas, George W., and James C. Miller III. *Economic Regulation of Domestic Air Transport: Theory and Policy.*
Noll, Roger G., ed. *Government and the Sports Business.*
Pechman, Joseph A., and Benjamin A. Okner. *Who Bears the Tax Burden?*

Foreign Policy Studies

Barnett, A. Doak. *Uncertain Passage: China's Transition to the Post-Mao Era.*
Binkin, Martin. *U.S. Reserve Forces: The Problem of the Weekend Warrior.*
Brown, Seyom. *New Forces in World Politics.*
Halperin, Morton H. *Bureaucratic Politics and Foreign Policy.*
Lawrence, Richard D., and Jeffrey Record. *U.S. Force Structure in NATO: An Alternative.*
Record, Jeffrey. *U.S. Nuclear Weapons in Europe: Issues and Alternatives.*
White, William D. *U.S. Tactical Air Power: Missions, Forces, and Costs.*

Governmental Studies

Derthick, Martha. *Between State and Nation: Regional Organizations of the United States.*
Hess, Stephen. *The Presidential Campaign: The Leadership Selection Process after Watergate.*
Mazmanian, Daniel A. *Third Parties in Presidential Elections.*

1975

Economic Studies

Aaron, Henry J. *Who Pays the Property Tax? A New View.*
Blechman, Barry M., Edward M. Gramlich, and Robert W. Hartman. *Setting National Priorities: The 1976 Budget.*
Bosworth, Barry, James S. Duesenberry, and Andrew S. Carron. *Capital Needs in the Seventies.*

Break, George F., and Joseph A. Pechman. *Federal Tax Reform: The Impossible Dream?*

Davis, Karen. *National Health Insurance: Benefits, Costs, and Consequences.*

Goodwin, Craufurd D., ed. *Exhortation and Controls: The Search for a Wage-Price Policy, 1945–1971.*

Gramlich, Edward M., and Patricia P. Koshel. *Educational Performance Contracting: An Evaluation of an Experiment.*

Jantscher, Gerald R. *Bread upon the Waters: Federal Aids to the Maritime Industries.*

Kneese, V. Allen, and Charles L. Schultze. *Pollution, Prices, and Public Policy.*

Lanzillotti, Robert F., Mary T. Hamilton, and R. Blaine Roberts. *Phase II in Review: The Price Commission Experience.*

McKie, James W., ed. *Social Responsibility and the Business Predicament.*

Okun, Arthur M. *Equality and Efficiency: The Big Tradeoff.*

Pechman, Joseph A., and P. Michael Timpane, eds. *Work Incentives and Income Guarantees: The New Jersey Negative Income Tax Experiment.*

Phillips, Almarin, ed. *Promoting Competition in Regulated Markets.*

Rivlin, Alice M., and P. Michael Timpane, eds. *Ethical and Legal Issues of Social Experimentation.*

Rivlin, Alice M., and P. Michael Timpane, eds. *Planned Variation in Education: Should We Give Up or Try Harder?*

Foreign Policy Studies

Bergsten, C. Fred, and Lawrence B. Krause, eds. *World Politics and International Economics.*

Binkin, Martin. *The Military Pay Muddle.*

Blechman, Barry M. *The Control of Naval Armaments: Prospects and Possibilities.*

Clough, Ralph N. *East Asia and U.S. Security.*

Clough, Ralph N., A. Doak Barnett, Morton H. Halperin, and Jerome H. Kahan. *The United States, China, and Arms Control.*

Fried, Edward R., and Charles L. Schultze, eds. *Higher Oil Prices and the World Economy: The Adjustment Problem.*

Greene, Fred. *Stresses in U.S.-Japanese Security Relations.*

Kahan, Jerome H. *Security in the Nuclear Age: Developing U.S. Strategic Arms Policy.*

Record, Jeffrey. *Sizing Up the Soviet Army.*

Toward Peace in the Middle East. Report of a Study Group.
Trezise, Philip H. *The Atlantic Connection: Prospects, Problems, and Policies.*

Governmental Studies

Beard, Edmund, and Stephen Horn. *Congressional Ethics: The View from the House.*
Derthick, Martha. *Uncontrollable Spending for Social Services Grants.*
Nathan, Richard P., Allen D. Manvel, Susannah E. Calkins, and associates. *Monitoring Revenue Sharing.*
Sundquist, James L. *Dispersing Populations: What America Can Learn from Europe.*

1976

Economic Studies

Aaron, Henry J., ed. *Inflation and the Income Tax.*
Caves, Richard E., and Masu Uekusa. *Industrial Organization in Japan.*
Denison, Edward F., and William K. Chung. *How Japan's Economy Grew So Fast: The Sources of Postwar Expansion.*
Goode, Richard. *The Individual Income Tax*, rev. ed.
Owen, Henry, and Charles L. Schultze, eds. *Setting National Priorities: The Next Ten Years.*
Owen, Wilfred. *Transportation for Cities: The Role of Federal Policy.*
Patrick, Hugh, and Henry Rosovsky, eds. *Asia's New Giant: How the Japanese Economy Works.*

Foreign Policy Studies

Binkin, Martin, and Jeffrey Record. *Where Does the Marine Corps Go from Here?*
Cline, William R. *International Monetary Reform and the Developing Countries.*
Clough, Ralph N. *Deterrence and Defense in Korea: The Role of U.S. Forces.*
Destler, I. M., Priscilla Clapp, Hideo Sato, and Haruhiro Fukui. *Managing an Alliance: The Politics of U.S.-Japanese Relations.*

Quanbeck, Alton H., and Archie L. Wood. *Modernizing the Strategic Bomber Force: Why and How.*
Trezise, Philip H. *Rebuilding Grain Reserves: Toward an International System.*

Governmental Studies

Hess, Stephen. *Organizing the Presidency.*
Kaufman, Herbert. *Are Government Organizations Immortal?*
Keech, William R., and Donald R. Matthews. *The Party's Choice.*
Stanley, David T. *Prisoners Among Us: The Problem of Parole.*
Steiner, Gilbert Y. *The Children's Cause.*

1977

Economic Studies

Brittain, John A. *The Inheritance of Economic Status.*
Krause, Lawrence, and Walter S. Salant, eds. *Worldwide Inflation: Theory and Recent Experience.*
Maxwell, James A., and J. Richard Aronson. *Financing State and Local Governments,* 3d ed.
Munnell, Alicia H. *The Future of Social Security.*
Ott, David J., and Attiat F. Ott. *Federal Budget Policy,* 3d ed.
Pechman, Joseph A. *Federal Tax Policy,* 3d ed.
Pechman, Joseph A., ed. *Comprehensive Income Taxation.*
Pechman, Joseph A., ed. *Setting National Priorities: The 1978 Budget.*
Schultze, Charles L. *The Public Use of Private Interest.*

Foreign Policy Studies

Barnett, A. Doak. *China and the Major Powers in East Asia.*
Barnett, A. Doak. *China Policy: Old Problems and New Challenges.*
Binkin, Martin, and Shirley J. Bach. *Women and the Military.*
Blechman, Barry M., and others. *The Soviet Military Buildup and U.S. Defense Spending.*
Brown, Seyom, and others. *Regimes for the Ocean, Outer Space, and Weather.*
Frank, Charles R., Jr. *Foreign Trade and Domestic Aid.*

Frank, Charles R., Jr., and Richard C. Webb, eds. *Income Distribution and Growth in the Less-Developed Countries.*
Tilton, John E. *The Future of Nonfuel Minerals.*

Governmental Studies

Heclo, Hugh. *A Government of Strangers: Executive Politics in Washington.*
Horowitz, Donald L. *The Courts and Social Policy.*
Kaufman, Herbert. *Red Tape: Its Origins, Uses, and Abuses.*
Nathan, Richard P., Charles F. Adams, Jr., and associates. *Revenue Sharing: The Second Round.*

1978

Economic Studies

Aaron, Henry J. *Politics and the Professors: The Great Society in Perspective.*
Brittain, John A. *Inheritance and the Inequality of Material Wealth.*
Davis, Karen P., and Cathy Schoen. *Health and the War on Poverty: A Ten-Year Appraisal.*
Okun, Arthur M., and George L. Perry, eds. *Curing Chronic Inflation.*
Palmer, John L., ed. *Creating Jobs: Public Employment Programs and Wage Subsidies.*
Palmer, John L., and Joseph A. Pechman, eds. *Welfare in Rural Areas: The North Carolina–Iowa Income Maintenance Experiment.*
Pechman, Joseph A., ed. *Setting National Priorities: The 1979 Budget.*
Weber, Arnold R., and Daniel J. B. Mitchell. *The Pay Board's Progress: Wage Controls in Phase II.*

Foreign Policy Studies

Bergsten, C. Fred, Thomas Horst, and Theodore H. Moran. *American Multinationals and American Interests.*
Berman, Robert P. *Soviet Air Power in Transition.*
Binkin, Martin. *Shaping the Defense Civilian Work Force: Economics, Politics, and National Security.*

Blechman, Barry M., and Stephen S. Kaplan. *Force without War: U.S. Armed Forces as a Political Instrument.*
Cline, William R., and Enrique Delgado, eds. *Economic Integration in Central America.*
Cline, William R., Noboru Kawanabe, T.O.M. Kronsjö, and Thomas Williams. *Trade Negotiations in the Tokyo Round: A Quantitative Assessment.*
Farley, Philip J., Stephen S. Kaplan, and William H. Lewis. *Arms across the Sea.*
Musgrove, Philip. *Consumer Behavior in Latin America: Income and Spending of Families in Ten Andean Cities.*
Sanderson, Fred H. *Japan's Food Prospects and Policies.*
Steinberg, Eleanor B., and Joseph A. Yager. *New Means of Financing International Needs.*

Governmental Studies

Breneman, David W., and Chester E. Finn, Jr., eds. *Public Policy and Private Higher Education.*
Finn, Chester E., Jr. *Scholars, Dollars, and Bureaucrats.*
Hess, Stephen. *The Presidential Campaign,* rev. ed.
Orfield, Gary. *Must We Bus? Segregated Schools and National Policy.*

1979

Economic Studies

Cooper, George. *A Voluntary Tax? New Perspectives on Sophisticated Estate Tax Avoidance.*
Denison, Edward F. *Accounting for Slower Economic Growth: The United States in the 1970s.*
McLure, Charles E., Jr. *Must Corporate Income Be Taxed Twice?*
Pechman, Joseph A., ed. *Setting National Priorities: The 1980 Budget.*
Russell, Louise B. *Technology in Hospitals: Medical Advances and Their Diffusion.*

Foreign Policy Studies

Binkin, Martin, and Irene Kyriakopoulos. *Youth or Experience? Manning the Modern Military.*

Gelb, Leslie H. *The Irony of Vietnam: The System Worked.*
Johnson, Stuart E. *The Military Equation in Northeast Asia.*
Lefever, Ernest W. *Nuclear Arms in the Third World: U.S. Policy Dilemma.*
Sanderson, Fred H., and Shyamal Roy. *Food Trends and Prospects in India.*
Trezise, Philip H., ed. *The European Monetary System: Its Promise and Prospects.*

Governmental Studies

Derthick, Martha. *Policymaking for Social Security.*
Mazmanian, Daniel A., and Jeanne Nienaber. *Can Organizations Change? Environmental Protection, Citizen Participation, and the Corps of Engineers.*

1980

Economic Studies

Aaron, Henry J., and Michael J. Boskin, eds. *The Economics of Taxation.*
Break, George F. *Financing Government in a Federal System.*
Bryant, Ralph C. *Financial Interdependence and Variability in Exchange Rates.*
Bryant, Ralph C. *Money and Monetary Policy in Interdependent Nations.*
Caves, Richard E., and Lawrence B. Krause, eds. *Britain's Economic Performance.*
Hartman, Robert W., and Arnold R. Weber, eds. *The Rewards of Public Service: Compensating Top Federal Officials.*
Krause, Lawrence B., and Sueo Sekiguchi, eds. *Economic Interaction in the Pacific Basin.*
Mitchell, Daniel J. B. *Unions, Wages, and Inflation.*
Pechman, Joseph A., ed. *Setting National Priorities: Agenda for the 1980s.*
Pechman, Joseph A., ed. *What Should Be Taxed: Income or Expenditure?*

Foreign Policy Studies

Destler, I. M. *Making Foreign Economic Policy.*
Hough, Jerry F. *Soviet Leadership in Transition.*
Yager, Joseph A., ed. *Nonproliferation and U.S. Foreign Policy.*

1981

Economic Studies

Aaron, Henry J., ed. *The Value-Added Tax: Lessons from Europe.*

Aaron, Henry J., and Joseph A. Pechman, eds. *How Taxes Affect Economic Behavior.*

Bradbury, Katharine L., and Anthony Downs, eds. *Do Housing Allowances Work?*

Breneman, David W., and Susan C. Nelson. *Financing Community Colleges: An Economic Perspective.*

Carron, Andrew S. *Transition to a Free Market: Deregulation of the Air Cargo Industry.*

Crandall, Robert W. *The U.S. Steel Industry in Recurrent Crisis: Policy Options in a Competitive World.*

Crandall, Robert W., and Lester B. Lave, eds. *The Scientific Basis of Health and Safety Regulation.*

Downs, Anthony. *Neighborhoods and Urban Development.*

Goodwin, Craufurd D., ed. *Energy Policy in Perspective: Today's Problems, Yesterday's Solutions.*

Lave, Lester B. *The Strategy of Social Regulation: Decision Frameworks for Policy.*

Lave, Lester B., and Gilbert S. Omenn. *Clearing the Air: Reforming the Clean Air Act.*

Okun, Arthur M. *Prices and Quantities: A Macroeconomic Analysis.*

Pechman, Joseph A., ed. *Setting National Priorities: The 1982 Budget.*

Foreign Policy Studies

Barnett, A. Doak. *China's Economy in Global Perspective.*

Barnett, A. Doak. *The FX Decision: "Another Crucial Moment" in U.S.- China-Taiwan Relations.*

Betts, Richard K., ed. *Cruise Missiles: Technology, Strategy, Politics.*

Binkin, Martin, and Irene Kyriakopoulos. *Paying the Modern Military.*

Bruton, Henry J. *The Promise of Peace: Economic Cooperation between Egypt and Israel.*

Cline, William R., and others. *World Inflation and the Developing Countries.*

Cline, William R., and Sidney Weintraub, eds. *Economic Stabilization in Developing Countries.*

Kaplan, Stephen S. *Diplomacy of Power: Soviet Armed Forces as a Political Instrument.*
Kaufmann, William W. *Defense in the 1980s.*
Quandt, William B. *Saudi Arabia in the 1980s: Foreign Policy, Security, and Oil.*
Yager, Joseph A. *International Cooperation in Nuclear Energy.*

Governmental Studies

Hess, Stephen. *The Washington Reporters.*
Kaufman, Herbert. *The Administrative Behavior of Federal Bureau Chiefs.*
Nathan, Richard P., and others. *Public Service Employment: A Field Evaluation.*
Reichley, A. James. *Conservatives in an Age of Change: The Nixon and Ford Administrations.*
Steiner, Gilbert Y. *The Futility of Family Policy.*
Sundquist, James L. *The Decline and Resurgence of Congress.*

1982

Economic Studies

Aaron, Henry J. *Economic Effects of Social Security.*
Baily, Martin Neil, ed. *Workers, Jobs, and Inflation.*
Bosworth, Barry P., and Robert Z. Lawrence. *Commodity Prices and the New Inflation.*
Bradbury, Katharine L., Anthony Downs, and Kenneth A. Small. *Urban Decline and the Future of American Cities.*
Carron, Andrew S. *The Plight of the Thrift Institutions.*
Haveman, Robert H., and John L. Palmer, eds. *Jobs for Disadvantaged Workers: The Economics of Employment Subsidies.*
Krause, Lawrence B. *U.S. Economic Policy toward the Association of Southeast Asian Nations: Meeting the Japanese Challenge.*
Munnell, Alicia H. *The Economics of Private Pensions.*
Pechman, Joseph A., ed. *Setting National Priorities: The 1983 Budget.*
Russell, Louise B. *The Baby Boom Generation and the Economy.*

Foreign Policy Studies

Bakhash, Shaul. *The Politics of Oil and Revolution in Iran.*
Barnett, A. Doak. *U.S. Arms Sales: The China-Taiwan Tangle.*

Berman, Robert P., and John C. Baker. *Soviet Strategic Forces: Requirements and Responses.*

Betts, Richard K. *Cruise Missiles and U.S. Policy.*

Betts, Richard K. *Surprise Attack: Lessons for Defense Planning.*

Binkin, Martin, and Mark J. Eitelberg. *Blacks and the Military.*

Hough, Jerry F. *The Polish Crisis: American Policy Options.*

Kaufmann, William W. *Planning Conventional Forces: 1950–80.*

Quandt, William B. *Saudi Arabia's Oil Policy.*

Governmental Studies

Brown, Lawrence D. *The Political Structure of the Federal Health Planning Program.*

Dommell, Paul R., and others. *Decentralizing Urban Policy: Case Studies in Community Development.*

Morris, Milton D., and Albert Mayio. *Curbing Illegal Immigration.*

Center for Public Policy Education

Fried, Edward R., and Henry D. Owen, eds. *The Future Role of the World Bank.* (Dialogues on Public Policy)

Smith, Bruce L. R., and James D. Carroll, eds. *Improving the Accountability and Performance of Government.* (Dialogues on Public Policy)

Also Published by Brookings

Head, Robert V. *Federal Information Systems Management: Issues and New Directions.*

1983

Economic Studies

Aaron, Henry J. *The Peculiar Problem of Taxing Life Insurance Companies.*

Bryant, Ralph C. *Controlling Money: The Federal Reserve and Its Critics.*

Carron, Andrew S. *The Rescue of the Thrift Industry.*
Crandall, Robert W. *Controlling Industrial Pollution: The Economics and Politics of Clean Air.*
Downs, Anthony. *Rental Housing in the 1980s.*
Flanagan, Robert J., David Soskice, and Lloyd Ulman. *Unionism, Economic Stabilization, and Incomes Policies: European Experience.*
Hartman, Robert W. *Pay and Pensions for Federal Workers.*
Keeler, Theodore E. *Railroads, Freight, and Public Policy.*
Lave, Lester B., ed. *Quantitative Risk Assessment in Regulation.*
Pechman, Joseph A., ed. *Setting National Priorities: The 1984 Budget.*
Tobin, James, ed. *Macroeconomics, Prices, and Quantities: Essays in Memory of Arthur M. Okun.*

Foreign Policy Studies

Dale, Richard S., and Richard P. Mattione. *Managing Global Debt.*
Fried, Edward R., Philip H. Trezise, and Shigenobu Yoshida, eds. *The Future Course of U.S.-Japan Economic Relations.* (Dialogues on Public Policy)
Garthoff, Raymond L. *Perspectives on the Strategic Balance.*
Hickman, William F. *Ravaged and Reborn: The Iranian Army, 1982.*
Mako, William P. *U.S. Ground Forces and the Defense of Central Europe.*
Schwartz, David N. *NATO's Nuclear Dilemmas.*
Steinbruner, John D., and Leon V. Sigal, eds. *Alliance Security: NATO and the No-First-Use Question.*

Governmental Studies

Anton, Thomas J. *Federal Aid to Detroit.*
Brown, Lawrence D. *New Policies, New Politics: Government's Response to Government's Growth.*
Brown, Lawrence D. *Politics and Health Care Organization: HMOs as Federal Policy.*
Fossett, James W. *Federal Aid to Big Cities: The Politics of Dependence.*
MacManus, Susan A. *Federal Aid to Houston.*
Melnick, R. Shep. *Regulation and the Courts: The Case of the Clean Air Act.*

Orlebeke, Charles J. *Federal Aid to Chicago.*
Schmandt, Henry J., George D. Wendel, and E. Allan Tomey. *Federal Aid to St. Louis.*
Steiner, Gilbert Y., ed. *The Abortion Dispute and the American System.*
Sundquist, James L. *Dynamics of the Party System: Alignment and Realignment of Political Parties in the United States,* rev. ed.

Center for Public Policy Education

Panem, Sandra, ed. *Public Policy, Science, and Environmental Risk.* (Dialogues on Public Policy)

1984

Economic Studies

Aaron, Henry J., and Gary Burtless, eds. *Retirement and Economic Behavior.*
Aaron, Henry J., and William B. Schwartz. *The Painful Prescription: Rationing Hospital Care.*
Bosworth, Barry P. *Tax Incentives and Economic Growth.*
Caves, Richard E., and Lawrence B. Krause, eds. *The Australian Economy: A View from the North.*
Downs, Anthony, and Katharine L. Bradbury, eds. *Energy Costs, Urban Development, and Housing.*
Goode, Richard. *Government Finance in Developing Countries.*
Lawrence, Robert Z. *Can America Compete?*
Pechman, Joseph A. *Federal Tax Policy,* 4th ed.
Rivlin, Alice M., ed. *Economic Choices 1984.*

Foreign Policy Studies

Binkin, Martin. *America's Volunteer Military: Progress and Prospects.*
Bohi, Douglas R., and William B. Quandt. *Energy Security in the 1980s: Economic and Political Perspectives.*
Carter, Ashton B., and David N. Schwartz, eds. *Ballistic Missile Defense.*
Cline, William R. *Exports of Manufactures from Developing Countries.*

Enders, Thomas O., and Richard P. Mattione. *Latin America: The Crisis of Debt and Growth.*
Fried, Edward R., and Philip H. Trezise, eds. *U.S.-Canadian Economic Relations: Next Steps?* (Dialogues on Public Policy)
Garthoff, Raymond L. *Intelligence Assessment and Policymaking: A Decision Point in the Kennedy Administration.*
Helms, Christine Moss. *Iraq: Eastern Flank of the Arab World.*
Hewett, Ed A. *Energy, Economics, and Foreign Policy in the Soviet Union.*
Kaufmann, William W. *The 1985 Defense Budget.*
Sigal, Leon V. *Nuclear Forces in Europe: Enduring Dilemmas, Present Prospects.*
Spindler, J. Andrew. *The Politics of International Credit: Private Finance and Foreign Policy in Germany and Japan.*
Weintraub, Sidney. *Free Trade between Mexico and the United States?*
Yager, Joseph A. *The Energy Balance in Northeast Asia.*

Governmental Studies

Brown, Lawrence D., James W. Fossett, and Kenneth T. Palmer. *The Changing Politics of Federal Grants.*
Hess, Stephen. *The Government/Press Connection: Press Officers and Their Offices.*
Liebschutz, Sarah F. *Federal Aid to Rochester.*

Center for Public Policy Education

Panem, Sandra. *The Interferon Crusade.*
Pechman, Joseph A., ed. *Options for Tax Reform.* (Dialogues on Public Policy)
Smith, Bruce L. R., ed. *The Higher Civil Service in Europe and Canada: Lessons for the United States.* (Dialogues on Public Policy)

1985

Economic Studies

Aaron, Henry J., and Harvey Galper. *Assessing Tax Reform.*
Carron, Andrew S. *Reforming the Bank Regulatory Structure.*
Denison, Edward F. *Trends in American Economic Growth, 1929–82.*
Downs, Anthony. *The Revolution in Real Estate Finance.*

Goode, Richard. *Economic Assistance to Developing Countries through the IMF.*
Guttentag, Jack M., and Richard J. Herring. *The Current Crisis in International Lending.*
Pechman, Joseph A. *Who Paid the Taxes, 1966–85?*
Russell, Louise B. *Is Prevention Better than Cure?*
Steuerle, C. Eugene. *Taxes, Loans, and Inflation: How the Nation's Wealth Becomes Misallocated.*

Foreign Policy Studies

Blair, Bruce G. *Strategic Command and Control: Redefining the Nuclear Threat.*
Epstein, Joshua M. *The Calculus of Conventional War: Dynamic Analysis without Lanchester Theory.*
Garthoff, Raymond L. *Détente and Confrontation: American-Soviet Relations from Nixon to Reagan.*
Grunwald, Joseph, and Kenneth Flamm. *The Global Factory: Foreign Assembly in International Trade.*
Kaufmann, William W. *The 1986 Defense Budget.*
Lindberg, Leon N., and Charles S. Maier, eds. *The Politics of Inflation and Economic Stagnation.*
Mattione, Richard P. *OPEC's Investments and the International Financial System.*
McNaugher, Thomas L. *Arms and Oil: U.S. Military Strategy and the Persian Gulf.*
Nacht, Michael. *The Age of Vulnerability: Threats to the Nuclear Stalemate.*

Governmental Studies

Chubb, John E., and Paul E. Peterson, eds. *The New Direction in American Politics.*
Derthick, Martha, and Paul J. Quirk. *The Politics of Deregulation.*
Morris, Milton D. *Immigration—The Beleaguered Bureaucracy.*
Peterson, Paul E., ed. *The New Urban Reality.*
Reichley, A. James. *Religion in American Public Life.*
Steiner, Gilbert Y. *Constitutional Inequality: The Political Fortunes of the Equal Rights Amendment.*
Weaver, R. Kent. *The Politics of Industrial Change: Railway Policy in North America.*

Center for Public Policy Education

Baily, Mary Ann, and Warren I. Cikins, eds. *The Effects of Litigation on Health Care Costs.* (Dialogues on Public Policy)

Levine, Charles H., ed. *The Unfinished Agenda for Civil Service Reform: Implications of the Grace Commission Report.* (Dialogues on Public Policy)

Smith, Bruce L. R., ed. *The State of Graduate Education.* (Dialogues on Public Policy)

1986

Economic Studies

Aaron, Henry J., and Cameran M. Lougy. *The Comparable Worth Controversy.*

Aaron, Henry J., and others. *Economic Choices 1987.*

Aronson, J. Richard, and John L. Hilley. *Financing State and Local Governments,* 4th ed.

Barnett, Donald F., and Robert W. Crandall. *Up from the Ashes: The Rise of the Steel Minimill in the United States.*

Crandall, Robert W., and others. *Regulating the Automobile.*

Kenen, Peter B. *Financing, Adjustment, and the International Monetary Fund.*

Lawrence, Robert Z., and Robert E. Litan. *Saving Free Trade: A Pragmatic Approach.*

Morrison, Steven, and Clifford Winston. *The Economic Effects of Airline Deregulation.*

Sawhill, John C., and Richard Cotton, eds. *Energy Conservation: Successes and Failures.*

Schultze, Charles L. *Other Times, Other Places: Macroeconomic Lessons from U.S. and European History.*

Foreign Policy Studies

Adams, William James, and Christian Stoffaës, eds. *French Industrial Policy.*

Binkin, Martin. *Military Technology and Defense Manpower.*

Epstein, Joshua M. *The 1987 Defense Budget.*

Hough, Jerry F. *The Struggle for the Third World: Soviet Debates and American Options.*

Kaufmann, William W. *A Reasonable Defense.*
Quandt, William B. *Camp David: Peacemaking and Politics.*

Governmental Studies

Hess, Stephen. *The Ultimate Insiders: U.S. Senators in the National Media.*
Katzmann, Robert A. *Institutional Disability: The Saga of Transportation Policy for the Disabled.*
Nivola, Pietro S. *The Politics of Energy Conservation.*
Peterson, Paul E., Barry G. Rabe, and Kenneth K. Wong. *When Federalism Works.*
Sundquist, James L. *Constitutional Reform and Effective Government.*

Center for Public Policy Education

Panem, Sandra, ed. *Biotechnology: Implications for Public Policy.* (Dialogues on Public Policy)

1987

Economic Studies

Bosworth, Barry P., and Alice M. Rivlin, eds. *The Swedish Economy.*
Bosworth, Barry P., Andrew S. Carron, and Elisabeth H. Rhyne. *The Economics of Federal Credit Programs.*
Brown, Clair, and Joseph A. Pechman, eds. *Gender in the Workplace.*
Bryant, Ralph C. *International Financial Intermediation.*
Burtless, Gary, ed. *Work, Health, and Income among the Elderly.*
Flanagan, Robert J. *Labor Relations and the Litigation Explosion.*
Lawrence, Robert Z., and Charles L. Schultze, eds. *Barriers to European Growth: A Transatlantic View.*
Litan, Robert E. *What Should Banks Do?*
Pechman, Joseph A. *Federal Tax Policy,* 5th ed.
Ravenscraft, David J., and F. M. Scherer. *Mergers, Sell-Offs, and Economic Efficiency.*
Russell, Louise B. *Evaluating Preventive Care: Report on a Workshop.*

Wiener, Joshua, ed. *Swing Beds: Assessing Flexible Health Care in Rural Communities.* (Dialogues on Public Policy)

Winston, Clifford, and others. *Blind Intersection? Policy and the Automobile Industry.*

Foreign Policy Studies

Betts, Richard K. *Nuclear Blackmail and Nuclear Balance.*

Carter, Ashton B., John D. Steinbruner, and Charles A. Zraket, eds. *Managing Nuclear Operations.*

Dickson, Bruce, and Harry Harding, eds. *Economic Relations in the Asian-Pacific Region.* (Dialogues on Public Policy)

Epstein, Joshua M. *The 1988 Defense Budget.*

Epstein, Joshua M. *Strategy and Force Planning: The Case of the Persian Gulf.*

Flamm, Kenneth. *Targeting the Computer: Government Support and International Competition.*

Fried, Edward R., Frank Stone, and Philip H. Trezise, eds. *Building a Canadian-American Free Trade Area.* (Dialogues on Public Policy)

Garthoff, Raymond L. *Policy versus the Law: The Reinterpretation of the ABM Treaty.*

Garthoff, Raymond L. *Reflections on the Cuban Missile Crisis.*

Gordon, Lincoln. *Eroding Empire: Western Relations with Eastern Europe.*

Harding, Harry. *China's Second Revolution: Reform after Mao.*

Kaufmann, William W. *A Thoroughly Efficient Navy.*

MccGwire, Michael. *Military Objectives in Soviet Foreign Policy.*

Stares, Paul B. *Space and National Security.*

Stern, Robert M., Philip H. Trezise, and John Whalley, eds. *Perspectives on a U.S.-Canadian Free Trade Agreement.*

Governmental Studies

Reichley, A. James. *Elections American Style.*

Center for Public Policy Education

Pechman, Joseph A., ed. *Tax Reform and the U.S. Economy.* (Dialogues on Public Policy)

Sevick, James R., and Warren I. Cikins, eds. *Constructing Correctional Facilities: Is There a Role for the Private Sector?* (Dialogues on Public Policy)

1988

Economic Studies

Aaron, Henry J., Harvey Galper, and Joseph A. Pechman, eds. *Uneasy Compromise: Problems of a Hybrid Income-Consumption Tax.*
Baily, Martin Neil, and Alok K. Chakrabarti. *Innovation and the Productivity Crisis.*
Bryant, Ralph C., and others. *Empirical Macroeconomics for Interdependent Economies.* 2 vols.
Bryant, Ralph C., Gerald Holtham, and Peter Hooper, eds. *External Deficits and the Dollar: The Pit and the Pendulum.*
Litan, Robert E., and Clifford Winston, eds. *Liability: Perspectives and Policy.*
Litan, Robert E., Robert Z. Lawrence, and Charles L. Schultze, eds. *American Living Standards: Threats and Challenges.*
Rivlin, Alice M., and Joshua M. Wiener. *Caring for the Disabled Elderly: Who Will Pay?*

Foreign Policy Studies

Flamm, Kenneth. *Creating the Computer: Government, Industry, and High Technology.*
Hewett, Ed A. *Reforming the Soviet Economy: Equality versus Efficiency.*
Hough, Jerry F. *Opening Up the Soviet Economy.*
Lincoln, Edward J. *Japan: Facing Economic Maturity.*
May, Michael M., George F. Bing, and John D. Steinbruner. *Strategic Arms Reductions.*
Quandt, William B., ed. *The Middle East: Ten Years after Camp David.*
Sahliyeh, Emile. *In Search of Leadership: West Bank Politics since 1967.*
Toward Arab-Israeli Peace: Guidelines for American Policy. Report of a Study Group.

Governmental Studies

Bach, Stanley, and Steven S. Smith. *Managing Uncertainty in the House of Representatives: Adaptation and Innovation in Special Rules.*

Hess, Stephen. *Organizing the Presidency,* rev. ed.
Hess, Stephen. *The Presidential Campaign,* 3d ed.
Katzmann, Robert A. *Judges and Legislators: Toward Institutional Comity.*
Weaver, R. Kent. *Automatic Government: The Politics of Indexation.*

Center for Public Policy Education

Fried, Edward R., and Nanette M. Blandin, eds. *Oil and America's Security.* (Dialogues on Public Policy)
Pechman, Joseph A., ed. *World Tax Reform: A Progress Report.* (Dialogues on Public Policy)

Also Published by Brookings

Conlan, Timothy. *New Federalism: Intergovernmental Reform from Nixon to Reagan.*

1989

Economic Studies

Aaron, Henry J., Barry P. Bosworth, and Gary Burtless. *Can America Afford to Grow Old? Paying for Social Security.*
Blueprint for Restructuring America's Financial Institutions. Report of a Task Force.
Bryant, Ralph C., and others, eds. *Macroeconomic Policies in an Interdependent World.* (Copublished with the International Monetary Fund and the Centre for Economic Policy Research)
Cooper, Richard N., and others. *Can Nations Agree? Issues in International Economic Cooperation.*
Crandall, Robert W., and Kenneth Flamm, eds. *Changing the Rules: Technological Change, International Competition, and Regulation in Communications.*
Denison, Edward F. *Estimates of Productivity Change by Industry: An Evaluation and an Alternative.*

202   B R O O K I N G S   A T   S E V E N T Y - F I V E

Justice for All: Reducing Costs and Delay in Civil Litigation. Report of the
Brookings Task Force on Civil Justice Reform.
Russell, Louise B. *Medicare's New Hospital Payment System: Is It Working?*
Small, Kenneth A., Clifford Winston, and Carol A. Evans. *Road Work: A New
Highway Pricing and Investment Policy.*

Foreign Policy Studies

Adams, William James. *Restructuring the French Economy: Government and the
Rise of Market Competition since World War II.*
Binkin, Martin, and William W. Kaufmann. *U.S. Army Guard and Reserve:
Rhetoric, Realities, Risks.*
Fried, Edward R., and Philip H. Trezise, eds. *Third World Debt: The Next
Phase.* (Dialogues on Public Policy)
Garthoff, Raymond L. *Reflections on the Cuban Missile Crisis,* rev. ed.
Kaufmann, William W., and Lawrence J. Korb. *The 1990 Defense Budget.*
McNaugher, Thomas L. *New Weapons, Old Politics: America's Military Procure-
ment Muddle.*
Pilling, Donald. *Competition in Defense Procurement.*
Steinbruner, John D., ed. *Restructuring American Foreign Policy.*

Governmental Studies

Chubb, John E., and Paul E. Peterson, eds. *Can the Government Govern?*
Smith, Steven S. *Call to Order: Floor Politics in the House and Senate.*

Center for Public Policy Education

Falco, Mathea, and Warren I. Cikins, eds. *Toward a National Policy on Drugs
and AIDS Testing.* (Dialogues on Public Policy)
Strosberg, Martin A., I. Alan Fein, and James D. Carroll, eds. *Rationing Medical
Care for the Critically Ill.* (Dialogues on Public Policy)

Also Published by Brookings

Bosworth, Barry P., and others. *Critical Choices: What the President Should Know About the Economy and Foreign Policy.*
Cook, Timothy E. *Making Laws and Making News: Media Strategies in the U.S. House of Representatives.*
Pechman, Joseph A. *Tax Reform: The Rich and The Poor,* 2d ed.

1990

Economic Studies

Aaron, Henry J., ed. *Setting National Priorities: Policy for the Nineties.*
Blinder, Alan S., ed. *Paying for Productivity: A Look at the Evidence.*
Burtless, Gary, ed. *A Future of Lousy Jobs? The Changing Structure of U.S. Wages.*
Lawrence, Robert Z., and Charles L. Schultze, eds. *An American Trade Strategy: Options for the 1990s.*
Shoven, John B., and Joel Waldfogel, eds. *Debt, Taxes, and Corporate Restructuring.*
Winston, Clifford, and others. *The Economic Effects of Surface Freight Deregulation.*

Foreign Policy Studies

An-Na'im, Abdullahi Ahmed, and Francis M. Deng. *Human Rights in Africa: Cross-Cultural Perspectives.*
Epstein, Joshua M. *Conventional Force Reductions: A Dynamic Assessment.*
Epstein, Joshua M., and Raj Gupta. *Controlling the Greenhouse Effect: Five Global Regimes Compared.* (Occasional Paper)
Garthoff, Raymond L. *Deterrence and the Revolution in Soviet Military Doctrine.*
Hufbauer, Gary Clyde, ed. *Europe 1992: An American Perspective.*
Kaufmann, William W. *Glasnost, Perestroika, and U.S. Defense Spending.*
Lincoln, Edward J. *Japan's Unequal Trade.*
Quandt, William B. *The United States and Egypt: An Essay on Policy for the 1990s.*
Stares, Paul B. *Allied Rights and Legal Constraints on German Military Power.* (Occasional Paper)

Governmental Studies

Aberbach, Joel D. *Keeping a Watchful Eye: The Politics of Congressional Oversight.*
Chubb, John E., and Terry M. Moe. *Politics, Markets, and America's Schools.*
Derthick, Martha. *Agency under Stress: The Social Security Administration in American Government.*
Magleby, David B., and Candice J. Nelson. *The Money Chase: Congressional Campaign Finance Reform.*
Mann, Thomas E., ed. *A Question of Balance: The President, the Congress, and Foreign Policy.*
Peterson, Paul E., and Mark C. Rom. *Welfare Magnets: A New Case for a National Standard.*

Center for Public Policy Education

Hauptman, Arthur M. *The Tuition Dilemma: Assessing New Ways to Pay for College.*

Also Published by Brookings

Hunter, James Davison, and Os Guiness, eds. *Articles of Faith, Articles of Peace: The Religious Liberty Clauses and the American Public Philosophy.*
Nothdurft, William E. *SchoolWorks: Reinventing Public Schools to Create the Workforce of the Future.* (A German Marshall Fund of the United States book)
Smith, Bruce L. R. *American Science Policy since World War II.*

Serials

A Brookings Bulletin, 1944–52
The Brookings Bulletin, 1962–82
The Brookings Review, 1982–
Brookings Papers on Economic Activity, 1970–
Brookings Papers on Economic Activity: Microeconomics, 1987–

APPENDIX B:
BOARD OF TRUSTEES, 1916–91

The following list includes the board members of the Brookings Institution and its predecessors: the Institute for Government Research, the Institute of Economics, and the Robert Brookings Graduate School of Economics and Government.

Chairmen

Robert S. Brookings	1928–32
Frederic A. Delano	1933–37
Dwight F. Davis	1937–45
Robert Perkins Bass	1946–49
William R. Biggs	1949–61
Morehead Patterson	1961–62
Eugene R. Black	1962–68
C. Douglas Dillon	1968–75
Robert V. Roosa	1975–86
Louis W. Cabot	1986–

Board Members

Edwin A. Alderman President, University of Virginia	1916–29

Robert S. Brookings   1916–32
Partner, Cupples Company

James F. Curtis   1916–25
Assistant Secretary of the Treasury;
Partner, Curtis, Fosdick & Belknap

R. Fulton Cutting   1916–25
Financier and Corporation Executive

Charles W. Eliot   1916–17
President, Harvard University

Raymond B. Fosdick   1916–31
President, Rockefeller Foundation;   honorary, 1966–72
Under Secretary General, League of Nations

Felix Frankfurter   1916–25
Associate Justice of the Supreme Court;
Professor, Harvard Law School

Frank J. Goodnow   1916–30
President, Johns Hopkins University

Arthur T. Hadley   1916–29
President, Yale University

Mrs. Edward H. (Mary W. Averell) Harriman   1916–17

James J. Hill   1916
President, Great Northern Railroad
System and Northern Securities Company

Cesar Lombardi   1916–19
Publisher, A. H. Belo and Company

A. Lawrence Lowell   1916–25
President, Harvard University

Samuel Mather   1916–31
Senior member, Pickands, Mather and
Company

William H. Taft   1920–25
President of the United States;
Chief Justice of the Supreme Court

Edwin F. Gay   1920–25
Dean, Graduate School of Business
Administration, Harvard University

Frederic A. Delano   1920–37
Member, Federal Reserve Board

Franklin K. Lane   1920–21
Secretary of the Interior

Silas H. Strawn   1920–25
Partner, Winston, Strawn & Shaw

Ray Lyman Wilbur   1920–25
Secretary of the Interior; President,
Stanford University

Richard B. Mellon   1921–25
President, Mellon National Bank

Whitefoord R. Cole   1922–25
President, Louisville and Nashville   1926–34
Railroad Company

Henry S. Dennison   1922–25
President, Dennison Manufacturing Company

David F. Houston   1922–34
Secretary of Agriculture; Secretary of the
Treasury; Chairman, Mutual Life Insurance
Company of New York; Chancellor, Washington
University, St. Louis

Charles L. Hutchinson   1922–24
President, Corn Exchange Bank

Norman H. Davis   1932–35
Member, International Monetary and
Economic Conference; Chairman, American
Delegation, Disarmament Conference, Geneva

Clarence Phelps Dodge   1932–39
Publisher, *Colorado Springs Gazette*

Morton D. Hull   1933–35
U.S. Representative from Illinois

Lessing Rosenthal   1933–49
Partner, Rosenthal, Eldridge, King
& Robbins

Harry Brookings Wallace   1933–55
Chairman, Cupples Company

John G. Winant   1934–47
Governor of New Hampshire; Ambassador
to Great Britain

Dwight F. Davis   1935–45
Secretary of War; Governor General of
the Philippine Islands

Alanson B. Houghton   1935–41
Ambassador to Germany; Ambassador to Great
Britain; Chairman, Corning Glass Works

Roland S. Morris   1935–45
Ambassador to Japan; Partner, Duane,
Morris & Heckscher

Anson Phelps Stokes   1935–46
Secretary, Yale University; President,
Phelps-Stokes Foundation

Robert Perkins Bass   1936–60
Governor of New Hampshire

Daniel W. Bell   1946–71
Under Secretary of the Treasury; President
and Chairman, American Security and Trust
Company

John J. McCloy   1946–47
U.S. High Commissioner for Germany;
President, Chase National Bank

John S. Dickey   1947–54
President, Dartmouth College

Leverett S. Lyon   1947–59
Chief Executive Officer, Chicago
Association of Commerce and Industry

Mrs. Robert S. (Isabel Vallé January) Brookings   1949–65

Colgate W. Darden, Jr.   1949–54
U.S. Representative from Virginia; Governor   1959–81
of Virginia; President, University of Virginia

John W. Hanes, Jr.   1949–55
Under Secretary of the Treasury;
Vice President and Director, Olin Industries

John E. Lockwood   1949–74
Consulting Partner, Milbank, Tweed,   honorary, 1974–
Hadley & McCloy

Lewis L. Strauss   1950–54
Chairman, Atomic Energy Commission;
Partner, Kuhn, Loeb and Company

Donald B. Woodward   1950–74
Vice President, Mutual Life Insurance
Company

Arthur Stanton Adams   1951–80
President, University of New Hampshire;
President, American Council on Education

Arthur H. Compton   1956–59
Dean, Division of Physical Sciences,
University of Chicago; Director, Metallurgical
Laboratory of the Manhattan Project; Chancellor,
Washington University, St. Louis

William C. Foster   1957–61
Under Secretary of Commerce; Deputy Secretary
of Defense; Executive Vice President and
Director, Olin Mathieson Chemical Corporation

Dillon Anderson   1958–74
Special Assistant to the President for
National Security Affairs; Partner, Baker,
Botts, Andrews & Shepherd

Morehead Patterson   1958–62
U.S. Representative, International Atomic
Energy Agency negotiations; Deputy
Representative, United Nations Commission on
Disarmament; Chairman and President, American
Machine and Foundry Company

Elliott V. Bell   1959–67
Superintendent of Banks, New York State;
Editor and Publisher, *Business Week*

Marion B. Folsom   1959–76
Secretary, Department of Health, Education,
and Welfare; Under Secretary of the Treasury;
Treasurer and Director, Eastman Kodak Company

Huntington Harris   1960–82
President, Press Intelligence, Inc.   honorary, 1982–

Sydney Stein, Jr.   1960–71
Partner, Stein Roe & Farnham   honorary, 1971–

Thomas H. Carroll II   1961–64
Vice President, The Ford Foundation;
President, George Washington University

C. Douglas Dillon   1965–75
Chairman of the Board and Director, U.S. &   honorary, 1975–
Foreign Securities Corporation; Secretary of
the Treasury

Vincent M. Barnett, Jr.   1967–84
James P. Baxter III Professor of History and Public   honorary, 1984–
Affairs, Williams College; President, Colgate University

John Fischer   1967–78
Editor-in-Chief and Executive Vice President,
Harper's Magazine, Inc.

J. Harvie Wilkinson, Jr.   1967–80
Chairman of the Board, State-Planters Bank
of Commerce and Trusts

Peter G. Peterson   1967–71
Chairman, Peterson & Jacobs, Inc.; Secretary
of Commerce; President, Bell & Howell Company

Kermit Gordon   1967–76
President, The Brookings Institution;
Director, Bureau of the Budget

Robert S. McNamara   1968–86
Secretary of Defense; President, The World   honorary, 1986–
Bank; President, Ford Motor Company

William McChesney Martin, Jr.   1970–76
Chairman, Board of Governors of the Federal   honorary, 1976–
Reserve System; Assistant Secretary of the
Treasury; Chairman of the Board, Export-Import
Bank; President, New York Stock Exchange

George M. Elsey   1971–83
President, The American National Red Cross;   honorary, 1983–84
Special Assistant to the Secretary of Defense

Barton M. Biggs   1975–84
Chairman, Morgan Stanley Asset Management, Inc.   honorary, 1984–

Bruce K. MacLaury   1977–
President, The Brookings Institution;
President, Federal Reserve Bank of
Minneapolis; Deputy Under Secretary of the
Treasury for Monetary Affairs

Bruce B. Dayton   1977–82
Chairman, Dayton Hudson Corporation;   honorary, 1982–
Chairman, Federal Reserve Bank of Minneapolis

Carla A. Hills   1977–81
United States Trade Representative;
Secretary of Housing and Urban Development

J. Lane Kirkland   1977–81
President, AFL-CIO

Charles W. Robinson   1977–84
Chairman, Energy Transition Corporation;   honorary, 1984–
Under Secretary of State for Economic Affairs;
Deputy Secretary of State

Lloyd N. Cutler   1977–79
Of Counsel, Wilmer, Cutler & Pickering;   1981–87
Counsel to the President   honorary, 1987–

John D. deButts   1978–81
Chairman of the Board, American
Telephone and Telegraph Company

James D. Robinson III   1978–
Chairman of the Board, American Express
Company

Frank T. Cary   1978–87
Chairman of the Board and Chief Executive   honorary, 1987–
Officer, IBM Corporation

Robert D. Haas   1982–
Chairman and Chief Executive Officer,
Levi Strauss & Company

Philip M. Hawley   1982–88
President and Chief Executive Officer,
Carter Hawley Hale Stores

Ralph S. Saul   1982–
Chairman, CIGNA Corporation;
President, American Stock Exchange

Howard R. Swearer   1982–
Director of the Institute for International
Studies, Brown University; President, Brown
University; President, Carleton College

Morris Tanenbaum   1982–
Vice Chairman and Chief Financial Officer,
American Telephone and Telegraph Company

Donald F. McHenry   1983–
Professsor of Diplomacy and International
Affairs, Georgetown University; U.S.
Permanent Representative to the United Nations

Samuel H. Armacost   1983–88
President and Chief Executive Officer,
BankAmerica Corporation and Bank of America
NT&SA

J. David Barnes   1983–88
Chairman and Chief Executive Officer, Mellon
Bank; President and Chief Executive Officer,
Mellon National Corporation

James D. Wolfensohn   1983–90
Chairman, John F. Kennedy Center for the   honorary, 1990–
Performing Arts; President, James D. Wolfensohn
Inc.; Executive Partner, Salomon Brothers

Maconda B. O'Connor   1986–89
President, The Brown Foundation

Richard G. Darman   1987–88
Director, Office of Management and Budget;
Managing Director, Shearson Lehman Hutton

B. Francis Saul II   1987–
Chairman, B. F. Saul & Company

Elizabeth E. Bailey   1988–
Professor of Economics, Industrial
Administration and Public Policy, Carnegie
Mellon University

Kenneth W. Dam   1988–
Vice President, Law & External Relations, IBM
Corporation; Deputy Secretary of State

D. Ronald Daniel   1988–
Director, McKinsey & Company, Inc.

Pamela C. Harriman   1988–

Thomas G. Labrecque   1988–
Chairman and Chief Executive Officer, Chase
Manhattan Corporation and Chase Manhattan Bank

Howard D. Samuel   1988–
President, Industrial Union Department,
AFL-CIO

Robert H. Smith   1988–
President, Charles E. Smith Construction,
Inc.

John C. Whitehead   1989–
Chairman, AEA Investors, Inc.; Deputy
Secretary of State

APPENDIX C:
FINANCIAL PROFILE, 1966–90

Total Operating Expenses, 1966–90

Millions of dollars

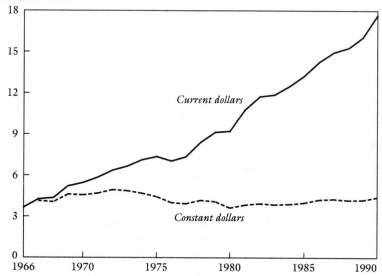

Endowment Market Value on June 30, 1966–90

Millions of dollars

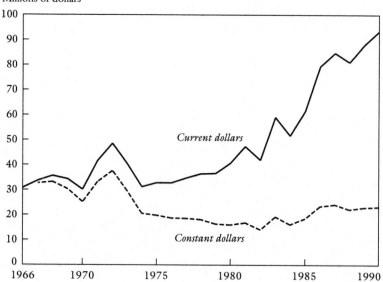

Operating Expenses by Program, 1966–90

Share of total

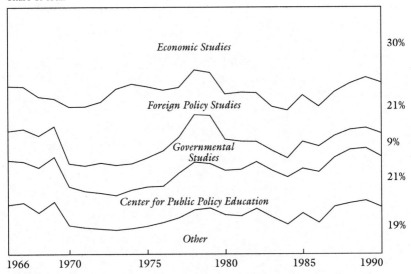

Economic Studies — 30%

Foreign Policy Studies — 21%

Governmental
Studies — 9%

Center for Public Policy Education — 21%

Other — 19%

1966   1970   1975   1980   1985   1990

Operating Revenue by Source, 1966–90

Share of total

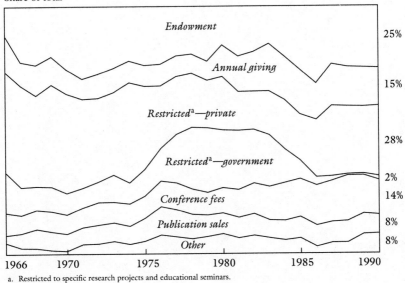

Endowment — 25%

Annual giving — 15%

Restricted[a]—private — 28%

Restricted[a]—government — 2%

Conference fees — 14%

Publication sales — 8%

Other — 8%

1966   1970   1975   1980   1985   1990

a. Restricted to specific research projects and educational seminars.

INDEX

AAA. *See* Agricultural Adjustment Administration (AAA)

Aaron, Henry J., 40, 77, 91, 100, 109, 146; experts and their political roles, 86–87; on taxation, 147; social science and, 87–88

Aberbach, Joel, 143

Ackley, Gardner, 78

Administration of Justice seminars, 125–26, 128

Advanced Study program, 53, 58, 119, 122–23; leadership education and, 124; neutral ground for informal exchange, 125; public policy conferences and seminars, 54; research contract program, 101; transition to CPPE, 126–27

Afghanistan, invasion of, 136

AFL-CIO, 124

Agency for International Development, 50, 107

Agnew, Spiro, 96

Agricultural Adjustment Administration (AAA), 27–28

Airline Deregulation Act (*1978*), 151

American Bar Association, 124

American Enterprise Institute, 54, 97, 115, 120, 135

American Management Association, 124

American Political Science Association, 143

Appalachian Regional Commission, 67

Arms Control and Disarmament Agency, 107

Asher, Robert, 43; foreign aid studies, 105–06; on Brookings hiring practices, 104

Baerresen, Donald, 53

Baker, James, 148

Balance of payments, U.S., 51–52

Balance-of-payments deficit, 149

Banking industry studies, 42, 152

Barnett, A. Doak, 105, 110, 160

Baruch, Bernard, 15

Beach, Walter, 120

Bell, Griffin, 126

Bergsten, C. Fred, 100, 104

Bernstein, Marver, 52

Betts, Richard K., 107–08, 155; strategic forces studies, 157–58; on weapons systems, 156
Binkin, Martin, 104; on defense program, 155; military manpower issues, 156
Black, Eugene D., 8
Blair, Bruce, 155; strategic studies, 157–58
Blechman, Barry, 104
Boskin, Michael, 147
Bosworth, Barry P., 135–36; on taxation policy, 148
Bradley, Bill, 148
Breyer, Stephen, 90
Bridge-building programs, 128–29
Brookings, Robert, Mrs.See January, Isabel Vallé
Brookings, Robert S., 12, 14, 24, 26, 40; better-trained civil servants and, 20–23; government and business careers, 15–16; on economic research, 17
Brookings Institution: American political middle ground and, 5, 100–11; analyzing capital formation, 30; balance-of-payment studies, 51; contract-research program, 27, 101, 113; criticism of New Deal programs, 25, 28, 30–31; educational programs and, 119–20, 127–29; fiftieth anniversary (1966), 1; financing and funding of, 7, 26–27, 54, 110–15; founding ideals, 10–15; governmental regulation of economic activity, 88–91; hostilities with Nixon administration, 96–98, 102; interaction with Congress and staffs, 75; liberal perception of, 95–96, 97, 101, 108; pseudonyms for, 94–95, 97; public policymaking process and, 6; publishing activity of, 81–82, 116–19, 153–54; rebuilding and relocation of, 40–45, 54; think tank image, 45–46; three-divisional organization, 41–42; Truman administration and, 34–35; unification and reorganization (1927), 22–23; university community and, 63–64, 92–93, 110, 117
Brookings Panel on Economic Activity, 81, 110
Brown, Lawrence D., 142
Brown, Seyom, 106

Bryant, Ralph C., 133; on international monetary policy, 149
Bryce, James, 69
Buchanan, Patrick, 96
Budget and Accounting Act (1921), 14, 82
Bureau of the Budget, 26, 82
Burger, Warren, 126
Burke, Edmund, 59
Burns, Arthur, 77
Burns, James MacGregor, 110

Calkins, Robert D., 39, 56, 58, 109–10; balance-of-payment studies and, 51–52; CPPE program and, 121; Keynesian background, 41; rebuilding Brookings and, 40–43, 53–55
Camp David accords, 133, 161
Cannon, Mark, 126
Capacity series, 29–30
Carnegie, Andrew, 16
Carnegie Corporation, 16, 17, 84
Carroll, James, 125; transition of Advanced Studies program and, 126–28
Carron, Andrew, 151
Carter administration, 86, 133, 135, 137, 150; block grant allocation formulas and, 73; Brookings staff and, 95
Cater, Douglass, 122
Caves, Richard, 92
Center for Advanced Study, 45
Center for Economic Progress and Employment, 152
Center for Public Policy Education (CPPE), 119, 123, 131; bridge-building programs, 128–29; creation of, 126–27; formal dedication (1985), 128; neutral ground for informal exchange, 125; workings and origin of, 120–21
Center for Strategic and International Studies, 54, 97, 115
Central Intelligence Agency, 129
Chase, Stuart, 25; liberal economics and, 31
China, 105, 160
Chubb, John E., 143
Cikins, Warren, 126
Civil Rights Act (1964), 71
Civil rights movement, 87

Civil Service Commission, 122–23
Clapp, Charles L., 52
Clark, Kenneth B., 61
Clean Air Act (*1970*), 150
Cleveland, Frederick, 11
Clough, Ralph, 105
Colson, Charles, 97
Commission on Economy and Efficiency, 10
Community Development Block Grants (CDBGs), 72–73
Comprehensive Employment and Training Act, 73
Conference Program on Public Affairs, 122
Conferences on Understanding Federal Government Operations (UFGOs), 123
Congressional Budget and Impoundment Control Act (*1974*), 85
Congressional Budget Office, 6, 85, 115
Congressional Research Service, 6, 115, 123
Conservatism, ascendance of, 134–35; Brookings and, 95–96, 137–38
Coolidge, Calvin, 27, 82
"Cooperative federalism," 49
Council of Economic Advisers (CEA), 18, 19, 33, 41, 57, 64, 78; balance-of-payment studies, 51; Brookings research projects for, 47; creation of, 58
CPPE. *See* Center for Public Policy Education (CPPE)
Crandall, Robert, 151–52
Cuban missile crisis, 160
Cummings, Milton C., Jr., 52
Cutting, R. Fulton, 12

David, Paul T., 43
Dean, John, 97
Defense Analysis Project, 104; funding for, 114
Defense budget studies, 156
Deficit, U.S., 51
Delano, Frederic A., 26, 27, 31
Denison, Edward, 92; economic growth, 146–47
Department of Commerce, 73
Department of Housing and Urban Development (HUD), 72

Department of Labor, 73
Deregulation studies, 151–52
Derthick, Martha, 64; Governmental Studies program and, 137; social security policymaking, 67, 142
Détente, policy of, 160
Doig, Jameson W., 52
Douglas, George W., 90
Downs, Anthony, 146

Eads, George, 90
Eastman, George, 21
Economic activity, publications on, 81–82
Economic Studies program, 41, 62, 145–46, 152; key policy advisers, 77
Eisenhower, Dwight David, 64, 65
Eisenhower administration, 43
Eliot, Charles W., 12
Ellsberg, Daniel, 96
Emergency Jobs Program Act (*1976*), 73
Employment Act of *1946*, 33
Environmental studies, 151
Epstein, Joshua M., 133, 155, 161; military defense budget, 156, 158
Ehrlichman, John, 97
European Community Institute for University Studies, 106
European Recovery Program, 37

Federal Executive Institute, 122
Federal Power Commission (FPC), 90
Federal Reserve, 111
Federal Training Act (*1958*), 122
Finn, Chester, 64
Flanigan, Peter, 98
Food and Drug Act (*1906*), 150
Ford administration, 101; block grant allocation formulas and, 73; conservative ideology and, 137
Ford Foundation, 42, 54, 57, 107; Center for Economic Studies and Progress, 152–53; funding for CPPE and, 120–21; governmental regulatory practices project, 88–89, 91; relationship with Brookings, 44, 47, 112–13; revenue sharing evaluation project, 71

Ford Motor Company, 128
Foreign aid studies, 103, 105
Foreign Policy Studies program, 41, 53, 102–03, 120; Brookings international affairs agenda, 155; Soviet Union studies and, 161; wider research audience and, 107
Foreman, Christopher H., Jr., 143
Fosdick, Raymond B., 40
France, 35
Frankfurter, Felix, 12
Fried, Edward R., 103, 133
Friedlaender, Ann F., 90
Friedman, Milton, 79
Fritschler, A. Lee, 125; Advanced Study program transition and, 126–28
Full Employment Bill, 35

Garthoff, Raymond, 160
Gelb, Leslie, 104; Pentagon Papers and, 96; on Vietnam, 107–08
George, Walter, 33
Germany, 33, 35
Goldman, Eric, 4
Goode, Richard, 48
Goodnow, Frank, 12
Goodrich, Leland, 43
Gorbachev, Mikhail, 159
Gordon, Kermit, 64, 83, 92, 95, 109, 110, 112; academic and government career, 56–57; Brookings political and ideological image, 99; director of Brookings, 57–60; doctrinal balance, 100; doctrine of governmental incapacity, 62–63; Economic Studies program and, 77–78; national agenda and, 60–62; on policy research, 75–76; relationship with Nixon administration, 96–98; Vietnam and, 102
Governmental Studies program, 41, 62, 142; democratic processes and bureaucracy, 70; directional change in, 63–64; framework of American institutions and, 143; government employment studies, 52–53; policymaking and policy outcomes, 67–68; Reagan revolution and, 137; research program for 1990s and,

143–44; school reform study, 141–42
Government Finance program, 47–48; tax studies, 48–50
Great Depression, 23, 66
Great Society programs, 2, 57, 135; categorical grant programs, 71; confused impact of, 60, 87; reappraisal of, 4
Greene, Jerome D., 11, 37
Greer, James, 43
Grunwald, Joseph, 53
Gurley, John G., 42

Hadley, Arthur Twining, 12
Haldeman, H. R., 96–97
Halperin, Morton, 104
Hamilton, Dean Walton, 21, 22
Hansen, Alvin, 41
Harding, Harry, 160
Harding, Warren G., 14, 82
Harriman, Mrs. Edward H., 12
Harris, Elisa D., 133
Harris, Joseph, 53
Hartley, Robert, 43
Hartman, Robert W., 91
Heclo, Hugh, 64; politics and civil service, 69
Held, Walter, 124, 125
Heller, Walter, 57, 71, 78
Henry, Laurin, 46
Heritage Foundation, 54, 115, 135
Hess, Stephen, 64, 100; culture of political journalism, 140–41; presidential selection and, 70
Hewett, Ed A., 159
Hill, James J., 12
Hoover, Herbert, 19, 25
Hoover commission, 122
Hoover Institution, 135
Hough, Jerry, 159
Housing and Community Act (1976), 73

Inflation, 34, 91, 135
Institute for Defense Analysis, 47
Institute for Government Research, 10, 18, 21, 22, 24, 37, 82; administrative effi-

ciency and, 12, 19, 35, 68; budget reform, 14; early work and publications of, 13; formal incorporation (*1916*), 11–12
Institute for Policy Studies, 54
Institute of Economics, 17, 21; research program in *1920s*, 19
Internal Revenue Service (IRS), 96, 147
International Bank for Reconstruction and Development, 36
International Monetary Fund, 36
International monetary system, 52
International payments deficit, 149
International Studies program, 35–36; goals definition of, 36–37
Interstate Commerce Act (*1887*), 88; deficiencies in, 90
"Invisible handshake," 80
Iran, 130, 160
Iraq, 132

January, Isabel Vallé, 21, 54
Japan, 33, 34; study of economy, 92
Japan Economic Research Center, 106
Jennings, M. Kent, 52
Johnson, Hugh, 25
Johnson, Lyndon Baines, 57, 65, 71, 78, 96, 101; Executive Order (*1966*), 82; speech at Brookings fiftieth anniversary, 2–4
Jones, Charles O., 143
Journalism community, 131–32; Hess study on, 140–41

Kaplan, A. D. H., 42
Kaplan, Stephen, 159
Katzmann, Robert A., 142–43
Kaufman, Herbert, 64; governmental bureaucracy studies, 68–70
Kaufmann, William, 103, 135; naval force use, 156; on nuclear forces, 136–37; on defense program, 155–56
Keech, William R., 70
Kennedy, John F., 2, 46, 57, 65, 101
Keynes, John Maynard, 41, 89
Keynesians, 32, 33, 41, 80
Kilpatrick, Franklin P., 52
Kipper, Judith, 133

Kissinger, Henry, 61
Korb, Lawrence J., 120, 125; invasion of Kuwait and, 134; military defense budget, 156
Krause, Lawrence, 92
Kristol, Irving, 79
Kuwait, invasion of, 132–33

Labor Studies Center, 124
Latin America, 50; economic integration studies, 53
Latin American studies, 161
Lave, Lester B., 150
Lawrence, Robert Z., 149
Lefever, Ernest W., 53
Leontieff, Wassily, 42
Lewis, Wilfred, Jr., 48
Lincoln, Edward J., 160–61
Lippmann, Walter, 30
Litan, Robert, 149–50, 151, 153; banking industry studies, 152
Littell, Barbara, 121
Living standards studies, 153
Lovett, Robert S., 15
Lowell, A. Lawrence, 12
Lubin, Isador, 19, 29
Lyon, Leverett, 28, 29

MacAvoy, Paul, 90
MccGwire, Michael, 155; naval force use, 156; on Soviet military doctrine, 159
McGovern, George, 70
McGowan, John, 90
MacLaury, Bruce K., 111–12, 138; Brookings fiscal problems and, 114–15; Brookings publishing activity and, 116, 119
McNamara, Robert, 82
McNaugher, Thomas L., 133, 155, 161; military procurement, 156
McPherson, Harry, 3
Malof, Peter, 124, 127
Manley, John, 64
Mann, Dean E., 52
Mann, Thomas, 142–43
Marcy, Carl, 43
Marshall Plan, 37

Matthews, Donald, 64; on presidential selection, 70
Maxwell, James A., 49
Meriam, Lewis, 35
Merrill Foundation, 57
Metz, Harold, 35
Middle East studies, 161
Military forces, analyses of, 158–59
Miller, James C. III, 90
Minarik, Joseph, 147
Mitchell, James M., 122–24
Mitchell, Wesley, 17
Moe, Terry M., 143
Mondale, Walter, 146
Monitoring Studies group, 71; public funding for employment and, 73
Morrison, Steven, 151
Moulton, Harold G., 18, 22, 25, 28, 38, 39, 58, 106; dangers of critical research and, 29; depression strategy for Brookings, 27; on federal bureaucracy, 35; market economy and, 31; on Keynesianism, 33–34
Moynihan, Daniel P., 64
Munnell, Alicia, 146

Nathan, Richard, 64, 97, 100; monitoring block grant funds under, 73; Nixon administration and, 71
National Bureau of Economic Research, 17, 47
National Commission for Manpower Policy, 73
National health insurance, 35
National Industrial Recovery Act (NIRA), 25, 30
National Recovery Administarion (NRA), 25, 27–28
National Resource Planning Board (NRPB), 33
National Science Foundation, 122
National security debates, 156–57
National Training and Development Service, 124
New Deal, 2, 29, 79, 135; Brookings Institution criticism of, 25, 27–28
New Federalism, 71; block grants and, 72

Newhouse, John, 104
New York Bureau of Municipal Research, 10, 11
Nivola, Pietro S., 142–43
Nixon, Richard Millhaus, 46, 64, 101; conservative ideology and, 137; New Federalism and, 71; social policy research and, 66–67; wage-price freeze, 81
Nixon administration, 100, 111; confrontation with Congress, 139; hostilities with Brookings, 96–99; school busing and, 67
Noll, Roger, 90
Norton, Charles D., 11
Nourse, Edwin, 18, 33; concurrent history and, 28
NRA. See National Recovery Administration (NRA)

Office of Economic Opportunity, 74
Office of External Affairs, 115
Office of Management and Budget, 6, 71, 83
Office of Price Administration, 41, 47, 56
Office of Strategic Services, 56
Office of Technology Assessment, 6, 115
Okner, Benjamin A., 147
Okun, Arthur M., 77, 79, 81, 86, 112, 159; aggregative economics and, 79–80; efficiency and equality trade-offs, 78–79; on new economics, 78
Omenn, Gilbert S., 150
Omnibus Judgeship Bill, 126
Orfield, Gary, 64; school busing studies, 67
Ott, Attiat F., 49
Ott, David J., 49
Owen, Henry, 102; Foreign Studies program and, 103, 107; hiring staff and, 104
Owen, Wilfred, 42; transportation research projects under, 50–51

Packwood, Robert, 148
Page, Thomas Walker, 19

Pasvolsky, Leo, 19, 29, 106; International Studies group and, 35–37
Patrick, Hugh, 92
Pechman, Joseph A., 40, 101, 112, 145; agenda for the *1980s* and, 135; Economic Studies program and, 77; on tax policy, 49–50, 147–48
Peck, Merton, 90
Pentagon Papers, 96, 107
Perkins, Donald, 152–53
Perry, George L., 81
Persian Gulf, 161
Peterson, Paul, 142
Planning, programming, and budgeting system (PPBS), 83
Policymaking and policy outcomes, 67–68
Policymaking environment, 6
PPBS. See Planning, programming, and budgeting system (PPBS)
Presidential elections and transition, 46–47, 59–60; intellectual migration and, 77
President's Commission on Personnel Interchange, 124
Pritchett, Henry, 17
Productivity growth studies, 154
Progressive Era, 1, 4, 53, 68, 138

Quandt, William, 133; Camp David accords, 161
Quirk, Paul, 142

Rand Corporation, 45, 47, 54, 116
Rawls, John, 79
Reagan, Ronald, 148; election in *1980*, 130
Reagan administration, 116, 120, 135; defense buildup, 155, 159; policy departures of, 146; revenue sharing and, 71; role of ideology and, 137; supply-side advocates, 147; tax reform and, 148
Regulatory studies, 88–91, 150–51
Reichley, James, 100; conservative resurgence and, 137; freedom in American society and, 138–39
Reischauer, Robert D., 91
Republican party, 25, 65

Revenue sharing, 71
Rhoades, Margaret, 131
Riesman, David, 121
Rivlin, Alice, 85–86, 118; Economic Studies program and, 145
Rockefeller, John D., 24
Rockefeller, Nelson, 64
Rockefeller Foundation, 11, 26; Brookings funding and, 36; Institute for Government Research and, 24; new Brookings building and, 44
Roosa, Robert, 111
Roosevelt, Franklin Delano, 25–26; reorganizing the executive office and, 31
Rosovsky, Henry, 92
Russell, Louise, 146
Russell, Ruth, 43

Sadowski, Yahya M., 133
Sady, Emil, 43
Salant, Walter, 41, 42, 51, 52
Saudi Arabia, 133, 161
Schick, Allen, 64
School busing and integration, 67
School reform study, 143
Schultze, Charles L., 77; budget deficit in the *1980s* and, 145–46; on federal budget, 84; on Vietnam, 61; outside political activities guidelines, 99–100; PPBS and political decisionmaking, 83; regulatory structures and, 91; on social science, 86
Schwartz, William B., 146
Scientific management, 10; Brookings Institution studies and, 30–31
Scranton, William, 137
Seidemann, Henry, 29
Setting National Priorities series, 84–85
Shaw, Edward S., 42
Shultz, George, 99
Simons, Anne, 43
Sino-American relations studies, 105, 160
Sloan Foundation, 81
Smoot-Hawley tariff, 19
Social economics and policy, 146
Social experimentation studies, 74
Social sciences, 82, 88; government funding for, 3–4; Kermit Gordon and, 59, 110;

policymaking in the *1970s* and, 86–87; professionalism in the *1920s*, 18
Social Security Administration, 29
Solow, Robert, 79
Sorkin, Alan, 91
Soviet Union, 35, 103, 154, 159–60
Stagflation, 4, 80
Standard Oil Trust, 24
Stanley, David, 52
Stares, Paul, 155
State Department, 47
Steinbruner, John, 155; national security issues and, 156–57; U.S.–Soviet relations and, 161–62
Steiner, Gilbert Y., 63, 70, 77, 111; on Brookings competition, 118; social policy research and, 66–67, 142
Stieber, Jack, 92
Stoessinger, John G., 53
Strategic forces and analysis, 157–58
Strategic parity, 103
Sundquist, James L., 61, 64, 137; on political institutions and, 139–40; political transformation and, 65–66
Supply-side economics, 147–48

Taft, William Howard, 10
Taft Commission, 14
Taft-Hartley Act, 35
Taxation studies, 48–50, 147–48
Tax Reform Act (*1969*), 98, 99
Tax Reform Act (*1986*), 148
Taylor, Frederick Winslow, 10
Technological change, 34
Tennessee Valley Authority, 67
Think tanks, 6–7, 94–95, 112, 131; Brookings and, 45; expansion in number of, 116
Tobin, James, 61, 78
Tocqueville, Alexis de, 9
Transportation projects, 47, 50; policy studies, 42
Transportation Research program, 50
Treasury Department, 72

Trezise, Philip, 100, 103
Tripartite Reports, 106–07
Truman, Harry, 25

United Auto Workers, 128
United Nations, 36; Brookings studies on, 37, 43, 53
Urban Institute, 54, 116
U.S.–Soviet relations, 161–62; strategic parity and, 103

Vaccara, Beatrice N., 42
Vail, Theodore, 12
Vandenberg, Arthur, 37
van Wise, Charles R., 12
Veblen, Thorstein, 30
Vietnam, 4, 60, 87, 96; foreign policy consensus and, 102

Wagner, Robert, 27
Wagner Act, 35
Walker Foundation, 81
War Industries Board, 15
Washington media, 132
Washington press corps, 140
Watergate affair, 87, 108, 140
Weaver, R. Kent, 142, 143
Wellington, Harry H., 92
White, Theodore, 5
Whitehead, Alfred North, 121
Wilcox, Francis, 43
Willoughby, William F., 13
Wilson, Harold, 56
Wilson, Woodrow, 10, 22
Winston, Clifford, 151–52
Winter, Ralph K., Jr., 92
Wood, Robert, 3
Woodward, Robert, 12
World War II, 102, 154; economists' war, 32